SPORTS PSYCHOLOGY AND INDIAN ATHLETES

A Psycho-physical Study

SPORTS PSYCHOLOGY AND INDIAN ATHLETES

A Psycho-physical Study

Maibam Chourjit Singh

AKANSHA PUBLISHING HOUSE
NEW DELHI • GUWAHATI • VISAKHAPATNAM

AKANSHA PUBLISHING HOUSE
4649-B/21, Ansari Road
Darya Ganj, New Delhi - 110 002
Ph.: 23263193 / 9811582579 / 09435116718
Fax: 011-23263193
Email: ektabooks@yahoo.com
www.akanshapublishinghouse.com

Sports Psychology and Indian Athletes: A Psycho-physical Study

First Published 2010
ISBN 978-81-8370-242-3

PRINTED IN INDIA

Published by Akansha Publishing House, New Delhi and Printed at Marmani Offset Press, Delhi.

To my beloved grandfather,

Late Shri Maibam Gouramani Singh

Former Transport Minister,
Government of Manipur

This book is humbly dedicated.

Contents

Preface

Sports psychology is an upcoming field of study these days. For better performance in the field of sports and games psycho-physical study of participants in various events may be guiding one. The present book makes an empirical psychophysical study of Indian athletes in general and Manipuri athletes in particular.

In spite of its diminutive size, remoteness and backwardness in economic development and growth, Manipur has had a long standing tradition in the field of games and sports with the influence of rich sports tradition. A rich heritage in sports includes the indigenous games like Thang–Ta (Martial Art), Mukna (Wrestling, Manipuri style), Shagol Kangjei (Manipuri Polo), Kang, Yubi Lakpi (similar to Rugby) and Khong Kangjei (similar to modern Hockey) etc. No doubt, contemporary history of games and sports in Manipur reveals an array of personalities in both national and international circuit.

Even though, we have rich culture of sports, there is great need of various studies in the field of physical education and sports. As we know that physical education is also part and parcel of sports, it is right time to enrich our sports literature. One of the problem is we have insufficient literature of sports.

Concerning the issue, the present book is an attempt to highlight the perspective of psychological and physical aspects of the athletes of Manipur. It is very essential to consider the athlete's psychological and physical fitness for the better enhancement of their performance. So, it is also important to investigate whether athlete's psycho-physical aspects is normal or not, or compatible to the highly competitive world of sports. The study of psycho-physical fitness will be helpful to all the person like physical education teacher, coaches, instructor as well as the administrator in order to know the weakness and strong points of their athletes. No doubt, this book will give the proper background for the systematic application of training methods.

Dr. Maibam Chourjit Singh

Acknowledgements

I would like to express my deep sense of gratitude and respect to my guide Dr. C.P. Singh, Associate professor, B.N. College of Physical Education, Udaipur for his inspiring guidance, constant support, Scholastic attitude and valuable suggestion in completing my work.

I express my thankfulness to Shri Tej Singh Shaktawat, Managing Director, B.N. Sansthan, Udaipur, Dr. B.L. Choudhary, Vice Chancellor, M.L.S. University, Dean (P.G.) Studies, M.L.S. University, Udaipur, Dr. A. Poonia, Dean Faculty of Education, M.L.S. University, Udaipur for providing me an opportunity to work on this study and facilities extended to me in carrying the same successfully.

Appreciation and Special thanks to Shri B.B. Sharma (I.A.S.), Director, Youth Affairs and Sports, Imphal, H. Udaychand Singh, Department of YAS and also President/ Secretary of the different sports Association of Manipur for letting me to collect the necessary data in a successful manner. Notwithstanding, I also thank Shri S. Tiken Singh, Director, Sports Authority of India (S.A.I.) Imphal for his kind support.

I am also thankful to the Coaches Mr. M. Deven Singh and Miss. Savitri Devi (Judo), Mr. A. Romi Sharma and Mangichand Singh (Sepak-Takraw), Mr. Maniratan and E. Ekendra Singh (Soccer), Mr. Hemjit Singh and Mr. Surjit Singh (Fencing), and Miss Sunita (Taekwondo) respectively for helping me to conduct the different tests with the full Cooperation of the athletes.

I am extremely grateful to Dr. N. Sharat Singh who took the major initiative in completing the statistical analysis of the data related with my study. Also, I am immensely grateful to Dr. S. Ranjit Singh and Dr. Kh. Rajen Singh, Lecturer, Dept. of Physical Education, D.M. College of Science, Imphal, Manipur for their kind and enthusiastic support all throughout my study. I again share my sincere gratitude to Mr. L. Robel Singh who helped me a lot in completing my work.

Grateful acknowledgement to Dr. Th. Kishan Singh, Lecturer, Dept. of English, D.M. College of Arts, Manipur and Dr. Madhavi Rathore, Dept. of English, B.N. Girls' College, Udaipur for the encouragement and better presentation of my study.

I once again thank my family members, relatives and friends specially Miss Reema Sinam for their guidance, support and encouragement in my entire study.

Sincere thanks are also expressed to the Library staff, M.L.S. University, Udaipur, Manipur University, Imphal, Lakshmibai National Institute of Physical Education, Gwalior, Siwaji University, Gwalior and Laboratory Assistants, SAI, Imphal for their Cooperation and possible assistance.

I am also rendering my warm regards to Mr. M.P.Misra, Akansha Publishing House, New Delhi for his sincere co-operation towards the publication of this book.

Lastly, but not the least, I express my appreciation to the athletes of Manipur who sincerely acts as subjects of this study, without whom it would not have been possible to complete this study.

Maibam Chourjit Singh

List of Tables

List of Figures

1

Introduction

Sports have become an indispensable part of our lives. The world of game and sports is ever expanding with intensity and competition. It also enhances scientific studies of human movements. Sports are dynamic and progressive in nature. It is not confined to "what has been" but its aim is to fix a new target. Sports performance is indeed an aspect of complex human performance. Hence, several disciplines of sports sciences are required to work in a co-coordinated manner to explain the nature of sports performance.

Psychology as a behavioral science has made its contribution for improving sports performance. An individual is only said healthy when he is physically fit, mentally sound, emotionally stable, and socially out-going. The total wellbeing of one's life depends up to a large extent upon his mental psyche. Sports psychology, as an applied psychology, is the greatest blessing of the modern day science in this age. Within a short span of time, sports psychology has taken giant strides. Singer states that "sports psychology explores one's behavior in athletics". Sports psychology, a new field of psychology, has come up very fast and is still progressing by leaps and bounds. It has helped coaches to coach more effectively and athletes to learn more efficiently. No training in the sports field is complete without reference to the psychological study and psychological training of athletes. Psychological conditioning of an athlete decidedly determines his success or failure in competitions. Most of the coaches agree that the physical characteristics, skills and training of the players are extremely important but they also indicate that good mental preparation for competition is a necessary component of success. A coach has the job of helping the athletes to find out his specific talents and factors for their fullest potential. This includes developing not only the physical attributes but also his psychological traits.

At present the psychological aspect have been emphasized and have become increasingly vital in the study of psychological characteristics that limits the performance of an individual in a given sports at high level of competition. Psychological readiness plays a decisive role as to determine whether or not an athlete in competitions and in training responds to his optimum potentials.

Psychological factors like Anxiety, Stress, Depression, Regression, Guilt, Fatigue, Extraversion and Arousal may cause negative performance or in other words performance may deteriorate. It is nothing but a state of mind in which the individual responds with discomfort to the events, that has occurred or is going to occur. The person's worries about events, their occurrences and consequences in general are the source of these factors. So, these psychological factors play a paramount role in sports. How an athlete handles the problem determines how successful he would be. The degree of these factors also varies with number of different conditions. It is likely to be greater in higher competitive sports, because in the competitive sports participants are under pressure to succeed. The study of the effect of the said psychological factors on sports performance has become a major topic of interest for sports psychologist in recent years.

Likewise, a close relationship exists between physical fitness and sports performance and in case the standard of games and sports in the country is to be improved, adequate stress will have to be laid on the enhancement of physical fitness status of our athletes. Even if an individual possesses high level of general motor ability, but lacks the basic necessary motor qualities, he may still be unable to perform well in particular sports unless he has developed a specific skill of that sport through long hours of practice. Strength, speed, endurance, agility, reaction time, speed of movement and coordination are the general components of the performance in the field of sports and games. General motor abilities assist a sportsman in learning specific skills and form a solid base, over which he can develop excellence in the particular game in which he is involved.

Physical fitness is directly related to the economic standard of a nation. Poor nation have poor standards of living and physical fitness. Physically fit persons can work hard and for longer hours at places of work and therefore give better outputs as compared to others. Not only this, the quality of the products also improves in such cases. Therefore, if we want to be called as developed nation we need to improve our physical fitness standards.

The pressures and tensions resulting from fast living have placed additional demand on our physical fitness. Adjust or perish is the law of nature. Therefore, in order to adjust ourselves to the changed demands of the times, we must improve our physical fitness levels. Growing cases of high blood pressure, heart failures, depressions and cancer etc. are indications that prove that we lacking our physical capacities to face such ailments. Growing particular malnutrition and population explosion have put additional pressures or our physical fitness. The need to lay more emphasis on our physical fitness levels, therefore, gains importance.

Physical fitness is important for an individual at every stage and in every walk of life. It is through physical fitness alone that he can enjoy a better life, which implies good education, satisfying occupation, social status and happiness. Physical fitness gives a distinct advantage to a person in this competitive world.

Physical fitness is a part of total fitness. It could be defined as the capacity of an individual to perform given physical task involving muscular efforts. The sensible organic ingredients of physical fitness include muscular power, muscular flexibility and neuro-muscular co-ordination. According to Barrow, physical health is a readiness or preparedness for performance with special regards for big muscle activity without undue fatigue.

Study of human body organs has gained new emphasis in the area of physical education and sports science also. Efforts are continuously made to study the body build of world class performance in different games and sports, so, any such attempt is very useful and justified in expanding the knowledge which could be applicable to select right type of individuals for particular games and sports and right type of games and sports for a particular individual. It is an accepted fact that the performance of an individual in games and sports has got a close relationship with his body built. On the basis of this, constant research programmes are taken up to find out the talented individual or a better performer. Each game has its requirement for certain physical and physiological components. The activities which are usually termed as body contact sports or games require considerable strength, power and fitness components.

Youth fitness is a topic of great national importance; yet adequate emphasis is not laid upon the development of physical, psychological and social fitness of Indian youths with reference to Manipur state of India. In spite of its diminutive size, remoteness and backwardness in economic development and growth, Manipur has had a long standing tradition in the field of games and sports. A rich heritage in this sphere includes a spectacular array of indigenous game like Thang-ta (Martial Art), Mukna (Wrestling), Shagol Kangjei (Polo), Kang, Yubi Lakpi (Rugby), Khong Kangjei (Hockey), etc. These games have enjoyed immense popularity amongst its people for ages. The internationally renowned game of Polo locally known as Shagol Kangjei originated in Manipur. Despite the crippling effects of immense underdevelopment, poverty, acute lack of infrastructure, prejudice and myopic policies, Manipur has seen an active interest in sporting activities all along. It is pertinent to point out the influence of tradition. Contemporary history of games and sports in Manipur reveals an array of personalities in both national and international circuits. Whether it may be individual events or team events, indoor or outdoor games, there is no dearth of sporting talent in Manipur. So, the central and state government should bear the responsibility for providing many opportunities for understanding and developing fitness in totality.

It is therefore obvious that there are a number of physical and psychological variables which contributes to the wholesome development of an athlete in the course of his performance. Hence, the study is undertaken to compare and to find the relationship between the psycho- physical health of athletes of Manipur at various levels.

Hypotheses

The hypotheses of the present investigation were as follows:-

1. There would be significant difference on physical health of the athletes of Manipur at various levels.

2. There would be significant difference on psychological health of the athletes of Manipur at various levels.
3. There would be no significant relationship between psychological health and physical health of the athletes of Manipur.

Definition and Explanation of the Terms

Athlete

An athlete is defined as a person possessing the natural or acquired traits, such as strength, agility and endurance that are necessary for physical exercise of sports, especially those performing in competitive content.

It is defined as a person trained in exercises of physical strength, speed and skill, especially one who participate or competes in games requiring agility and stamina.

Anxiety

Anxiety means apprehension, tension or uneasiness from anticipation of danger; the source of which is largely unknown or unrecognized or which is the emotional response to a consciously recognized and usually external threat or danger.

Anxiety is a state of mind in which an individual responds with discomfort to the event that has occurred or is going to occur.

Stress

It is defined as condition, or feeling experienced when a person perceives that demands exceeds the personal and social resources the individual is meant to mobilize.

It means any event or situation that makes heightened demands on a person's mental or emotional resources.

Depression

Depression means a mental state of excessive sadness characterized by persistently low mood, loss of interest and pleasure.

It is defined as a very lonely, frustrating and soul-destroying condition that requires support from friends, family, the medical profession, and community at large.

Regression

It is defined as a return to an earlier mental state, especially to infantile, patterns of thought of behavior, characteristics of many mental disorders also exhibited by normal persons in many situations.

It is also defined as the tendency of the quantitative traits of offspring to be closer to the population mean than their parent's trait.

Guilt

Guilt is defined as an emotion resulting from doing what one conceives of as wrong, thereby violating super age percepts; results in feelings of worthlessness and at times the need of punishment.

It means remorse caused by feeling responsible for some offence.

Fatigue

Fatigue means the decreased capacity or complete inability of an organism, an organ or a part to function normally because of excessive stimulation or prolonged exertion.

Fatigue means physical or mental weariness resulting from exertion.

Extraversion

It means the act, state or habit of being predominantly

concerned with an obtaining gratification from whatever is outside the self.

It is defined as a state in which attention and energies are largely directed outward from the self as opposed to inward toward the self.

Arousal

It is defined as a state of activation, either behavioral or physiological.

It is also defined as a feeling of apprehension or fear of which the source of this uneasiness is not always known or recognized, which can add to the distress one feels.

Height

Height is defined as a vertical dimension of extension; distance from the base of something to the top.

Height is defined as the vertical distance of a level, a point or an object considered as a point measured from specified datum, e.g. above ground.

Weight

Weight is defined as a quality of being heavy; the property by which bodies tend towards the centre of the earth; the effect of gravitational force, especially when expressed in certain units of standards.

Weight is defined as a quality representing the force exerted on a particle or object by an acceleration field, particularly the gravitational field of earth at the surface.

Agility

Agility may be defined as the ability of the body or the parts of the body to change directions rapidly and accurately.

Agility is the physical ability which enables an individual to rapidly change the body position and direction in a precise manner.

Cardio-Respiratory Endurance

It is defined as the kind of physiological fitness demonstrated through an adjustment of the heart and lungs to prolonged physical exertion.

It is defined as maximal amount of work that an individual can perform over an extended period of time.

Explosive Strength

Explosive strength is the ability of a muscle or a group of muscles to release minimum force in the shortest possible time, in an explosive manner, projecting the body or an object.

Explosive strength is the ability to keep the muscle fibre turned on for an extended period of time against the resistance.

Speed

Speed may be defined as the capacity of the individual to perform successive movement of the same position at fast rate.

It has also been defined as the capacity of the individual to perform successive movements of the same pattern at the rate which is fast and of a high order.

Strength

Strength is defined as force that a muscle or group of muscle can exert against a resistance in one maximum effort.

Strength is also defined as the capability of overcoming a certain resistance or of acting, against it by muscular tension (the term capacity here is used in the sense of functional potential).

Delimitations

1. The scope of the study was delimited to the athlete of the following games:

i) Soccer
ii) Sepak – Takraw
iii) Taekwondo
iv) Judo and
v) Fencing.

The subject of the study was confined to the selected athletes of the state of Manipur only.

Limitations

The physical health test conducted at play grounds with the help of trained persons, coaches and experts at different time variations (i.e. day, month, etc.) which has some effects on the performance of subject was considered as the limitation of the study.

Psychological health due to behavior dynamics that was affected with time was also considered as the limitation of the study.

Significance of the Study

The finding of the study will help in highlighting future investigators to explore the field of psycho-physical health of the athletes of Manipur at various levels. The result of study will also help the coaches and physical education teachers to guide their players in selecting the right games.

Therefore, the study would make the following contributions:-

The finding of the study will be helpful to policy makers in understanding the relationships of varying levels of physical and psychological health of athletes.

The study will also provide significance in motivating other researchers to take up similar studies with some other variables and different games and at different states.

The result of the study will also be helpful in evaluating Manipur state curriculum with respect to physical and psychological health of the athlete at various levels.

2

Review of Related Literature

The review of related literature is divided into two sections; that is reviews related to psychological health in section I and reviews related to physical health in section II. Thus, reviews related to the present study given in this chapter are cited as follows.

I: Review Related to Psychological Health

Adedoja administered the anxiety scale questionnaire designed by the Institution of Personality and Anxiety Testing for 31 colleges' physical education male students at Eastern Illinois University. The level of aspiration (Loa) scores was obtained from each student's estimate of performance on the groups' strength test. The 'p' of 16 indicated that there was no relationship between Loa and anxiety students. There was no difference between high and moderate or moderate and low anxiety. High moderate and low anxiety group did not differ in estimating the achievement scores to be above or below their actual scores on the strength test.

Aldrich and Edward combined several learning practice and motivation with the Erickson psychological development theory to examine the possible impact on academic achievement. The research questions were designed to discover if positive solution of the various psychological stages had possible relationship with study practices, achievement test score and grades.

Case studies of ninth grade students were developed. These students were of similar academic ability and background. Two had been identified as being better than expected than two who were not doing as well as expected.

The conclusion was that positive resolution of three stages Psychological Development are related to academic performance and study strategy practices was tentatively reached. Those stages were Autonomy versus Shame and doubt; Initiative versus Guilt, Industry versus Inferiority. There seemed to be some indication that early positive resolution of the identified stages resulted in the development of self regulation, metacognitive practices and academic achievement.

Collete, Nicholas and Kareng examined the relationship between an abusive family environment and proneness to shame, guilt, anger and hostility in college students, drawing on scale and inventory data from 280 undergraduates. Results revealed that greater exposure to emotional abusiveness was significantly related to higher shame, overt and covert hostility expressed to anger. Greater exposure to physical abusiveness was significantly related to hostility and tendency to experience anger without a specific provoking situation. Women reported higher shame and guilt, whereas men reported higher level of overt hostility and expressed anger. Shame proneness was related to covert hostility and unexpressed hostility to exposure and family abusiveness or on exception, to the anger and hostility variables.

Debnath conducted a study on psychological profiles of national women gymnasts and concluded that: (1) gymnast belonging to sub junior category were observed to be less intelligent, sober, venturesome, tough minded, (2) the junior gymnasts were observed to be less intelligent, sober, venturesome, tough minded, imaginative, controlled and relaxed, (3) The gymnasts belonging to the senior category were found to be sober, conscientious, tough minded, suspicious, imaginative experimenting relaxed.

Kim and Sook investigated the effect of taekwondo practice on psychological functioning of school children and adults. Ninety adult taekwondo practitioners, fifty-five primary school children, and sixty- one high school students participated in a series of two cross-sectional studies and two longitudinal studies. The two longitudinal studies focused on evaluating the practical significance of taekwondo exercise in school environments in promoting psychological health of school children.

The results showed that physiological workload of taekwondo is comparable with running at a speed of 9 km/ hr-1 and is classified as moderately heavy exercise which is effective in bringing about cardio-vascular training effects in healthy young adults. The result from the longitudinal studies showed that school children after participating in an extended taekwondo training program experienced less state and trait anxiety, mood disturbance, and significantly improved levels of emotion regulation. These results suggested that taekwondo can be used as an effective intervention in promoting both physical and psychological health of young people.

Leons Wilfred studied selected anthropometric characteristics and physical fitness components which contribute to the Judo performance. The subjects were 80 male Judo players of the Indian Inter-University, Kurukshetra in the year 1990. Eighty male judo players were selected, ten from each of the eight weight categories up to the first tenth position. The study concluded that the anthropometric variables were related to judo performance in various weight categories, but leg length, arm length, thigh girth and crucial ratio were not seen significantly related to judo performance in any other weight categories. Physical fitness variables were found to be significantly related to judo performance in various weight categories. However shoulder strength, leg strength, back strength and grip strength were not showing any significant relation with Judo performance.

Pintu Modak, determined the comparative effect of induced mental and physical fatigue on selected psychomotor tasks at various age levels. 120 male gymnasts of three different age levels i.e. beginners, state level and national / international, level (40 in each group) were selected at random from Calcutta and north eastern states of India. The data was collected after inducing the mental fatigue using standard test and physical fatigue using bicycle ergo meter for different durations. The mental fatigue for 10 minutes duration and 20 min duration were induced to group 'A' and group 'B' respectively. Similarly, the physical fatigue for 10 minutes duration and 20 min duration were induced to group 'C' and group 'D' respectively. One way analysis of variance was endeavored to determine the comparative effect of mental and physical fatigue of different durations on the performance of psycho motor tasks at different age level. Analysis of variance showed significant difference between the four groups among the beginners on the selected psycho-motor tasks.

Neaman and Dalerose compared relaxation techniques and visual motor behavioral rehearsal to determine which if either is more effective than an attention placebo intervention in reducing anxiety and enhancing performance in female gymnastic competition for 9-16 year. An experimental study was conducted, and 50 gymnasts, ages 9–16 who were competitors in the Kansas gymnastic association, levels five through nine were administered the Kansas self - evaluation.

These tests were used to assess anxiety prior to competition. The Judge's scores were tabulated to evaluate performance levels.

Prasana K investigated psychological factors influencing female participation in physical activities. The subjects from the study were selected at random from different levels of females belonging to different schools, colleges, and institutions of Kerala and Madhya Pradesh states. Eight hundred females belonging to four levels. Seventh to ninth class (N=200), tenth to twelve (N=200), graduates (N-200) and wording class (N=200), ages ranged from twelve to fourteen years, fifteen to seventeen years, eighteen to twenty two years and twenty to forty years respectively. The findings indicated that the psychological factors have significant effect on participation of females in physical activities. It also reveals that the psychological factors influencing the participation of females in physical activities differ at various levels.

Results predicted a relationship between a gymnast's anxiety and her performance was supported. It was predicted that relaxation training would reduce anxiety levels and enhance performance of the gymnast. This was supported for all events except pole vault. It also predicted that Visual Motor Behavioral Rehearsal (VMBR) training would result in greater levels of performance enhancement and anxiety reduction than would relaxation training on its own or attention – placebo was in the predicted direction.

Nou and Moh studied to identify processes by which social structured factors, stressors, and mediators affect mental health and life satisfaction among a large sample of Khmer University, college and technical students in modern Cambodia. The respondents for the study (N=1,257) were selected through a non-randomized stratified sampling procedure and recruited by institutional authority figure that selected a 10% opportunistic sample of students from respective departments by gender ratio and year at eleven Cambodia private, public and technical academic institutions. The study's findings consistently showed that both negative live events and daily hassles are significant predictors of higher mental health symptoms; higher psychological and somatic symptoms lower life satisfaction. The results further showed that for mental health symptoms status and psychological and somatic sub-dimensions, gender and social status are not significant predictors except that higher social status students had greater life satisfaction.

Smith and Randy studied relationship of anger and anxiety with depression. Many theories pose associations between anger and depression, yet have experienced difficulties in explicating this relationship. It is believed that difficulty is the result of the theoretical treatment of the constructs. Historically, theoretical treatment of anger and depression has been undimensional with each individual focusing on specific aspects of the construct depending on the theoretical stance of the observer. A cluster analysis with 281 participants was performed using instruments to assess depression, anger and anxiety. The current study explicated a number of relationship between anger and depression and suggested a need to develop a multidimensional understanding of depression and related affective state.

Liweiz has discussed the developing trend of China's sports psychology. It was pointed out that in the field of competitive sports psychology small sample study, experimental study, the developmental sports, oriented psychological testing, instruments, talented selection by psychological means, coaches, education of sports psychology and developmental sports, psychology should be paid close attention.

Seiler presented psychological performance enhancement training as predicted, taking into account the requirement and pre-requisites, the target population, the specific uses, and the severally applied training schedules. Future directions in psychological performance enhancement training are suggested with respect to the need for evaluation and practical considerations.

Swain and Jones conducted a study which examined the relationship between sports achievement orientation and cognitive anxiety, somatic anxiety and self-confidence on a sample of male (N=6) track & field athletes. Subjects responded to the competitive anxiety inventory (CSAI -2) on five occasions during the pre competition period and also completed the sports orientation questionnaire [8SQ]. In the case of cognitive anxiety, the high competitive group showed a progressive increase as the competition neared. Finding for somatic anxiety revealed that the low competitive group reported as earlier elevation in the somatic response. Significant main effects of both time-to-event and group (but no interaction) were found for self-confidence.

Nandi made a study on anxiety and its effect on performance on soccer skill and concluded that low anxiety subject performs significantly better than high anxiety subjects in dribbling the ball for time ends, kicking the ball for distance with left foot and performed well in gross motor soccer skill than those who were having low anxiety state.

II: Review Related to Physical Health

Agashe and Karkare aimed to identify the difference of motor fitness between tribal and non-tribal sports persons. 150 tribal boys (average age 15 – 53 years) and non-tribal boys (average age 15 – 26 years), 150 tribal girls (average age 15 – 34 years) and 150 non-tribal girls (average age 14 – 20 years) are selected as sample. All tribal samples are selected from Kride Parisar of Chhatisgarh State. Modified J.C.R. motor fitness test prepared by Cooper (1965) was administered to each subject. Results revealed that both tribal boys and girls were having significantly high speed and agility (p0<0.01). In vertical jump tribal boys were superior (p0<0.01). No difference was found on this dimension in tribal girls and non-tribal girls. Regarding chin-up tribal boys showed significantly more strength compared to non-tribal boys (p0<0.01), but surprisingly non-tribal girls were superior in chin-up item compared to tribal girls. Results indicated that tribal boys and girls were much more fit than non-tribal boys and girls in motor fitness.

Alan J. Pearce et al. studied to investigate and identify anthropometrical and physical performance differences between players who were selected in the final squad of one junior Australian Rules football club to those who were not selected. Fifty four junior ARF players were assessed using a battery of ARF standard anthropometric, height and weight, and physical performance tests, 20m straight-line speed, planned agility course, vertical jump power, and 3km endurance time-trial. Comparisons were made using MANOVA (significance $p<0.05$). Further analysis was completed to investigate if age was an influencing factor in selection. MANOVA showed significant differences between selected and non-selected players when height, mass, sprint, agility, and vertical jump were considered collectively. However, univariate analysis revealed that the vertical jump was the only significant individual test differentiating between selected

Amusa selected 46 colleges level football players and tested for running, speed, power, agility, maximum VO_2, strength, anaerobic capacity and flexibility in addition eleven anthropometric measurement consisting of skin fold and body diameters were taken. Soccer playing ability served as criteria and was measured by the rating of three experienced soccer coaches based on selected soccer skills and strategies. Analysis of data by zero order correlation and multiple R analysis resulting in the following conclusion. Maximum VO_2 and running speed are considered important factors in soccer performance, flexibility, agility, lactate concentration and leg power are not considered as valid indicators of playing ability.

Beiter studied 46 players who served as subjects for the construction of a football prediction test using general and specific motor performance tests. The 18 test included measurement of strength, power, speed, agility and body composition. All raw data were converted to T-score, multiple regression analysis selected the top 4 test to estimate the sum of 18 T-scores. Neither the 4 nor 18 item profile significant predicted started in the spring game multiple regression to predicted coaching rating (mean of 5 coaches) produced and R=66 using 1RM bench press power clean seven skin fold, blocking RT and Margacia Valama anaerobic power. The test battery developed in the study did not distinguish between starter and non starter possession of speed, strength and size. It does not guarantee success in a highly skilled game such as football.

Campbell studied 40 male members of the 1978 Spring Field College Varsity football squad and were tested for height, weight, 10, 20, 30 and 40 yard dash, speed, vertical jump, agility, upper body strength and lateral movement. In addition each player had a game performance score assessed by the grading of a game film selected at random data were treated by multiple "r" and regression "r". No relationships were found between height and weight and performance nor between agility and performance. Speed was found to relate positively to performance. It was concluded that performance in football cannot be effectively predicated by combination of the structural and physical performance variables utilized in the study.

Dasgupta P.K. and Mukhoupadhyay A.K. studied selected short distance runners, middle distance runners and long distance runners who were subjected to gradation on a treadmill. The maximum aerobic power (vo_2 max) and other indices related to deeper transport system viz. heart rate, ventilation volume, breathing reserve, dysprosic index, O_2 pulse and RQ were recorded at respective vo_2; maximum work loads and values were compared. Long distance runners and middle distance runners showed a significantly higher VO_2 maximum, than the short distance runners when VO_2, VO_2 maximum was expressed per unit body weight. Among the endurance runners, long distance runners had a significantly lower resulting pulse rate as well as the maximum heart rate during work than the middle distance runners. On comparison ventilation volume, breathing reserve, dysposic index, VO_2 pulse and RQ at VO_2 maximum work loads do not differ significantly among different categories of runners.

Dey and Debray studied the growth and development of cardio-respiratory and musculo-energetics systems. They investigated peak oxygen consumption (VO_2) and its relation to other anthropometric parameters of school boys (age 8-14 yrs.) from eastern region (ER) and north east region (NER) of India. This study also attempted to find out the effects of regional variation, including growth and development in comparison with the boys of other countries. The present study was carried out on 394 boys of 8-14 years of age, from the three different states of ER and five states of the NER on the Indian subcontinent. The results showed that the body size and peak view VO_2 of the boys from both regions increased significantly from 8-14 years of age. Peak VO_2 of the subjects was less than untrained Japanese, European and American boys. The weight related and lean body weight related peak VO_2 also changed from 8 years to 14 years boys in both the regions. It was also observed that peak VO_2 was also significantly and negatively correlated with a sum of skin fold thickness. Body size and peak VO_2 were found to be significantly higher in the ER boys than their NER counterparts at 13 and 14 years of age only. Peak VO_2 remained the same up to 12 years of age and then became significantly higher in the ER boys at 13 and 14 years of age as compared with their ER and NER counterparts. It was concluded that there was a significant difference in peak VO_2 of children from ER and NER.

Haley explained the effect of age on physical performance of elementary school boys in grade 1 through 6. 30 subjects were randomly selected from each class. The age of subjects ranged from 5 years 9 months to 12 years 2 months. 12 tests were conducted to test motor performance of the subjects. The study showed that motor performance score which increased with age and flexibility tended to decrease with age.

Leszek et al. investigate the correlation between general and special fitness of young football players, and their playing position on 20 selected football players with 6-year training experience constituted the subjects of their research. International Fitness Test was used to evaluate general physical fitness, and Football Abilities Test was used to evaluate special fitness. The analysis of the results showed that according to the classification of International Fitness Test's norms, the players were placed in the 320 – 480 point brackets, that defined their general physical fitness as medium. In the special fitness test the strikers definitely dominated, whereas the defensive players gained the poorest results. Spearman's rate correlation indicated statistical significance ($p<0,05$) in some tests. Research on the special and general physical fitness confirms interdependence rate and the influence on the level of football player.

Nakarmi and Bawa conducted an investigation with a purpose to determine significant differences, if any, in the physical abilities level of Nepalese Gymnastics girls with a training age of only 3 months and Nepalese school girls of

10-13 years of age. The study has been conducted on 34 subjects (17 girls Gymnasts and 17 school girls) who were students of same class and school in Kathmandu. To ascertain the physical abilities level measuring test that is shoulder rotation, back extension, trunk flexion, split sitting (fang), standing broad jump, vertical jump, push-ups, sit-ups and grip-strength were administered on each subject. Analysis of the data revealed that Nepalese gymnastic girls possess significantly better trunk flexibilities, hip flexibilities, leg explosive strength, arms and shoulder strength and abdominal strength when compared with the Nepalese school girls. The results also revealed non-significant differences in shoulder flexibility and grip strength between the two groups. Prakash conducted a comparative study on selected physiological and physical fitness factors of soccer and cricket player of 15 players each for the group of student undergoing special coaching in soccer and cricket were selected. Criterion measures selected were vital capacity, maximum expiratory breath holding capacity, maximum expiratory pressure, pulse rate, systolic blood pressure, diastolic blood pressure and speed (50 yard dash) shoulder girdle, explosive strength (soft ball throw) leg explosive strength (standing broad jump) muscular endurance (sit up) and flexibility (low touch in long lift position). He concluded that in well conditioned collegiate soccer players seen to have potential to develop cardio pulmonary fitness, muscular endurance as measured by chin-ups and explosive leg power by standing broad jump more than cricket players.

Prakash conducted a comparative study on selected physiological and physical fitness factors of soccer and cricket player of 15 players each for the group of student undergoing special coaching in soccer and cricket were selected. Criterion measures selected were vital capacity, maximum expiratory breath holding capacity, maximum expiratory pressure, pulse rate, systolic blood pressure, diastolic blood pressure and speed

(50 yard dash) shoulder girdle, explosive strength (soft ball throw), leg explosive strength (standing broad jump), muscular endurance (sit up) and flexibility (toe touch in long lift position). He concluded that in well conditioned collegiate soccer players seen to have potential to develop cardiopulmonary fitness, muscular endurance as measured by chin-ups and explosive leg power by standing broad jump more than cricket players.

Robins conducted a normative study for Albana students in 1 to 9 classes. About 2,545 boys and girls aged 6 to 14 years old, were given AAHPER youth fitness test and AAHPERT health related fitness test. Percentile tables were constructed for each item and based on age and sex, Albana and national means were compared. Albana students scored better on events measuring agility, speed and cardio-vascular endurance but the national score in abdominal, muscular endurance and flexibility was better.

S. Singh, J. Singh and H. Singh conducted a study to see the difference between fitness of senior and junior (girls) hockey players. The subject for this study were hockey girls attending the camp at SAINSNIS, Patiala. Five tests were administered to assess the physical fitness level. The data was statistically analyzed. It was found that there is no significant difference between senior and junior group in 30 mts. and standing broad jump test performance. The junior group was found to be significantly better in shoulder strength.

Thomas constructed a specific test battery of motor fitness for hockey players. He took 45 intercollegiate hockey players of Jiwaji University, Gwalior. The multiple correlations yielded five specific motor fitness tests namely, speed, endurance, power, flexibility and agility which are deemed to be meaningful in representing the specific motor fitness of hockey players. All the five tests (200 m run, six point run, two hand medicine balls throw, trunk flexion, and curt agility) showed high significant relationship with hockey playing ability to predict the specific motor fitness of hockey players.

Z. Borysiuk in his work presents detail analysis of somatic. Psychomotor, special and psychologic parameters of fencers during initial, directed and master stage of the training. Using specific statistical methods (facto and regressive analyses-Hellwig's model) agents determining the sports fitness were identified (n=65). Averages of height and body mass as well as slender index according to Reohar were calculated basing on age and registered somatic features. The test like fencing endurance, speed and special coordination, motorial adaptation and motion frequency capacity were performed. The procedure was enriched within the psychological examination through temperamental features measurement – Strelau Temperament Inventory (STI) and personality dimension – Eysenck Personality Questionnaire (EPQ). The analysis was conducted the specific fencing ability. Statistical significance was found in the following variables – fencing endurance, movement precision and motorial adaptation. In the final conclusion, comparative analyses of 3 examined groups showed that during the initial stage of training the physical fitness of fencers plats an important role while during the directed and master phase of practice the technical abilities development and psychomotor parameters grow more important.

3

Methodology

In conducting research, the method or procedure adopted is very important. The source of data, selection of subject, size, tools, administration of tools, collection of data, reliability of data and design of the study must be adopted. In this study the researcher has adopted the following procedures.

Source of Data

The present study has taken to the athletes from various games viz. fencing, soccer, taekwondo, sepak-takraw and judo who have participated in the district, state, national and international levels. The players are from different parts of Manipur.

Selection of Subjects

The subjects were selected from different districts of Manipur. The age of the subjects taken into consideration were from seventeen to twenty-three years. The locale of the present study was confined to 200 athletes of Manipur state. The sample was selected through purposive method of sampling. The subjects were selected from the following games viz., fencing, soccer, taekwondo, sepak-takraw and judo. It was divided into four different groups comprising of 50 athletes each in the district, state, national and international levels. From each level 10 subjects were selected representing altogether 40 subjects from one particular game.

Table - 1
Design of the Study

Game	*level of participation*				
	District	*State*	*National*	*Inter-national*	*Total*
Soccer	N=10	N=10	N=10	N=10	N=40
Sepak-takraw	N=10	N=10	N=10	N=10	N=40
Taekwondo	N=10	N=10	N=10	N=10	N=40
Judo	N=10	N=10	N=10	N=10	N=40
Fencing	N=10	N=10	N=10	N=10	N=40
Total	N=50	N=50	N=50	N=50	N=200

Selection of Variables

Based on the expert's opinion, availability of related literatures and feasibility of the test used, the following variables were selected for the present study. They are as follows:

- Psychological Health: (Anxiety, Stress, Depression, Regression, Fatigue, Guilt, Extraversion and Arousal).
- Physical Health: (Height, Weight, Agility, Cardio-Respiratory Endurance, Explosive Strength, Muscular Endurance, Speed and Strength Endurance).

Reliability of Data

Before starting the actual collection of data for all these variables, the reliability of data was ensured by establishing the instrument reliability, reliability of tests and subjects' reliability.

Instrument Reliability

To measure the psychological health, Eight State

Questionnaire [8SQ] was used. It is also a standardized test prepared by Barton, Cattell and Curran and their reliability was found to be very high.

For the measurement of physical health, the test items like 12 minute Run and Walk, 50 meter Dash and 10 meter Shuttle Run; the 400 meter standard track (synthetic track constructed by Germany) which is located at Khuman Lampak Sports Complex, Imphal was used.

Besides, instruments like stop watch, steel tape, stadeometer and electronic weighing machine (for the measurement of height and weight) used in this study were obtained from the standard firms which cater to the need of various research laboratories, sports departments or institutions in India and abroad. Their calibration is accepted as accurate enough for the purpose of the study. All the instruments were taken from Youth Affairs and Sports Department, Khuman Lampak and Sports Authority of India, N.E. region with prior permission from their respective officials.

Reliability of the Test

Psychological Health

The test, Eight State Questionnaire [8SQ] used for the psychological health in this study was also a standardized test having a high reliability.

Table – 2
Reliability of the Variables (8SQ)

Variable	Reliability
Anxiety	0.91
Stress	0.95
Depression	0.96
Regression	0.94
Fatigue	0.92
Guilt	0.96
Extraversion	0.96
Arousal	0.92

Physical Health

For the physical fitness, a standardized test called AAHPER Youth Fitness Test was sued. This test also possessed high reliability.

Table – 3

Reliability of the Variables (AAHPER)

Test items	*Reliability*
1. Pull up	0.95
2. Bent Knee Sit-ups	0.89
3. Standing Broad Jump	0.94
4. Shuttle Run	0.90
5. 50 meter Dash	0.92
6. 12 Minute Run Walk	0.94

Subjects' Reliability

For the present research, the subjects were given assurance that their responses would be kept confidential and would not be used for any other purposes except the present study so that they would be honest, frank and open without any fear. They performed at their best level with full enthusiasm and cooperation.

Procedure of Collection of Data

The necessary data were collected through various measuring tools. All the required data were collected with the permission from the Directorate of Youth Affairs and Sports, Sports Authority of India, N.E. Region and Clubs/ Associations. The data regarding the physical fitness was collected at their respective coaching centers mainly at Khuman Lampak Sports Complex which is located at Imphal, Manipur. The data regarding psychological health were collected through standardized questionnaires at their respective places of availability.

Tools

The selection of the test was based on the expert's opinion, administrative feasibility, time factor, nature of the subjects and facilities available to conduct the test. Thus, three standardized tests were used which are as follows:

Psychological Health

For the measurement of psychological health, the Eight State Questionnaire [8SQ] was used which is originally prepared by Barton, Cattell and Curran. It mainly emphasized on the eight psychological emotions namely anxiety, depression, regression, fatigue, guilt, extraversion and arousal of an athlete. The test comprised of 96 objective type questions covering eight sections which include all the above mentioned eight psychological status. Further, these eight sections consisted 12 questions each having four options viz. A, B, C and D and is scored either 0, 1, 2 or 3. The score of each item contributes to only one factor total. Since there are 12 items for each psychological factor, the highest possible raw score for each one of the variables mentioned above is 36.

Physical Health

The physical fitness levels of the athletes were measured with the help of AAHPER Youth Fitness Test. The test consisted of six items for the measurement of six different physical fitness components of the athlete. Here, the details of fitness battery items and components are given below –

1. Pull up - Shoulder muscular strength
2. Bent knee sit-ups - Strength endurance
3. Standing Broad jump - Explosive strength
4. Shuttle Run - Agility
5. 50 meter Dash - Speed
6. 12 minute run/walk - Cardio-respiratory endurance.

Administration of Tools

The officials of the different sports associations, Youth Affairs and Sports Department, Sports Authority of India (SAI) and individual athletes were contacted personally. The officials of the associations and departments were requested to allow their athletes to serve as the subjects of this study besides including the individual athletes. The research made sincere efforts to get true responses from the subjects. When they were free enough to fill up the questionnaire and perform the test items, the researcher met the athletes of the respective associations and departments at the practice area of the respective games especially during their practice sessions. For psychological health, since tests were to be administered through questionnaires all the necessary guidelines and instructions to be followed during the test were given. Meanwhile, the researcher also tried to convince the subjects by promising to send a separate abstract of the conclusion of the investigation to the concerned coaches and officials. They were also assured that their responses would be kept confidential and would not be used for any other purposes except the present study so that they would share an honest response without any fear. The required copy of the questionnaire for along with the answer sheet for psychological health were given to each one of them with further instructions to answer all the questions. Likewise for physical health also the test items were administered during their practice session with the supervision of the respective coaches. Thus, the standardized tools for the different variables were administered through the following ways.

Psychological Health

The eight state questionnaires [8SQ] along with the answer sheet were distributed to the subjects. Likewise as the procedures for SES, the necessary instructions and assistance were given to the subjects except that a limited time period of 25 minutes were given to fast or advanced readers and 35 minutes to slow or week readers in completing the questionnaires.

Physical Health

Regarding physical health the AAHPER Youth Fitness Test was administered to the necessary athletes. Administration of the test was conducted strictly in accordance with the procedure laid in the AAHPER Youth Fitness manual. All the items of the test were administered during their practice session. The test items were explained by the scholars along with their respective coaches and thus the athletes performed at their best levels. Since most of the athletes were used to the daily physical exercises, there were no troubles in conducting the said physical test. The test items administered are as follows:

Pull-up test

Objective: The objective of the test was to measure the muscular endurance of the arms and shoulder girdle in pulling the body upward.

Equipment: The equipment needed was a horizontal bar (1 and ½ inches in diameter) raised to a height so that the tallest performer cannot touch the ground from the hanging position.

Direction: The performance assumed the hanging position with the overhead grasp (palm forward) and pulled his body up ward until the chin was over the bar. After each chin-up he should return to fully extended hanging position. The subjects were not permitted to kick, jerk or use kick motion.

Scoring: The number of completed pull-up was recorded as the score of this test.

Bent Knee Sit Ups

Objective: The objective of the test was to measure the endurance strength of the abdominal muscle.

Equipment: A clear floor or mat and a stop watch were used.

Direction: Each subjects performed as many sit-up as he could do in one minute, in the manner described below:

The subject assumed a supine laying position with knees bent at an angle of less than 90 degree and feet or the floor with heels not more than 80 centimeter from the buttocks, and hands clasped behind neck. The feet were held down by a partner. To perform sit ups, the subject brought his head and elbows forward as he curled up touching elbows to the knees. In returning to the supine position it was ensured that elbows touched the floor every time.

Scoring: The number of completed sit-ups in one minute was recorded as the score for this test.

Standing Broad Jump

Objectives: The objective of the test was to measure the explosive power of the legs in jumping forward.

Equipment: Mat or outdoor jumping pit and measuring tape was used.

Direction: A take off line was drawn near one edge of the jumping pit. The subject was asked to take his position with toes just behind the take off line and feet slightly apart. Taking off both the feet simultaneously, he jumped to cover the maximum horizontal distance landing on both feet. While jumping he was asked to crouch slightly and swing the arms to aid the jump. Three trials were given and the best of three jumps was recorded as the standing broad jump performance.

Scoring: The score was horizontal distance measured in meters and centimeter to the nearest centimeter between the take off line and the nearest point where any part of the body touches the ground.

Shuttle Run

Objective: The objective of the test was to measure agility of the performers in running and changing direction.

Equipment: Two wooden blocks of 2x2x4 inches, stopwatch and measuring tape were used.

Direction: Two parallel lines were marked on the track/ ground 10 meters apart. Two wooden blocks were placed behind the restarting (opposite line). Each subject positioned himself behind the starting line and on the signal "go" he ran to the opposite end line, picked up a block, ran back to the standing line and placed the block behind it. He then repeated the process with the second block.

Scoring: The score for each performance was the length of time required (to the nearest length of a second) to complete the course. Two trials were allowed with some rest between the gap and the better timing was recorded as the score of this test items.

50 Meters Dash

Objective: The objective of the test was to measure the speed of the performer in running.

Equipment: Materials used are the clapper, stopwatch and 50 meter distance.

Direction: Two parallel lines were marked on the track or ground at 50 meters distance from each other one of these served as the starting line and the other the finish line.

It was advised that two subjects were start at the same time with a clapper and the time keeper for each subject recorded the time taken to cover the distance of 50 metres. The subjects ran as fast as possible across the finish line and trial was permitted.

Scoring: The elapsed time from the starting signal until the runner crossed the finish line was measured to the nearest tenth of a second.

12 Minutes Run/Walk: (As an option given in the AAHPER Youth fitness test manual, the 600m run or walk was replaced by 12 minute run and walk.

Objective: The objective of the test was to measure the cardio-respiratory endurance.

Equipment: 400 meter standard track, stopwatch, whistle, distance markers were all used.

Direction: Spotters were assigned for each runner. The runner started behind a line and upon the starting signal ran or walked as many laps as possible around the course within 12 minutes. The spotter maintained a count of each lap and when the signal to stop was given, they immediately ran to the spots which their runners were at the instant the whistle or command to stop was given.

Scoring: The score in meters as determined by multiplying the number of completed laps plus the number of segments (quarters, eight, 10 meter intervals, etc.) of an incomplete lap places the numbers of meter stopped off between a particular segment.

Note: Track was divided into quarter or segments of 50m by placing market and again within the segments it was distributed into 10m interval in order to measure the incomplete lap.

Example: The 12 minute run was given or a 400 m track sectioned of into eight and subject completes 5 laps plus 3 eight segments plus 10 meters. Then the subjects score is 5x400=2000; plus 3x50=150; plus 10 meters; i.e. 2000+150+10=2160 meters in 12 minutes.

Height

This tests is not included in the AAHPER Youth Fitness Test but used for the purpose of this study only.

Objective: The objective of the test was to measure the height of the athlete.

Equipment: Stedeometre

Direction: The subject was advised to stand in an erected position on the flat surface at the base of the Stedeometre with his head just below the sliding calibrated rod with hinged top piece. The top piece was fixed forming a right angle according to the height of the subjects and the reading was taken.

Scoring: The vertical distance from the base of the Stedeometre to the fixed calibrated rod measured in centimeter was taken as the score.

Weight: This test is also not included in the AAHPER Youth Fitness Test but used for the purpose of this study only.

Objective: The objective of the test was to measure the total body weight of the athlete.

Equipment: Electronic weighing machine.

Direction: The subject was advised to stand on the scale of the weighing machine wearing minimum cloths so that accurate body weight could be observed. The subject stood in an erected position with the feet totally touched on the scale. The subject remained in that position for a few seconds and the reading was noted.

Scoring: The final stoppage of raised indication as shown on the machine was recorded as the score of this test.

Statistical Analysis

The classical statistics –r, t, ANOVA-F, Levene's F., etc.

are utilized through SPSS (ver. 11.5). These tests are performed on the average score values of physical health and psychological health of the athletes of Manipur at four different levels – district, state, national and international. The analyses for investigating the variations in the indicators of interest are also furnished according to five different games–fencing, soccer, sepak-takraw, taekwondo and judo. The levels of significance of the tests are quantified at 0.05 and 0.01 probability levels.

4

Analysis of Data and Results

The analyses of the present study have been furnished through SPSS (Statistical Package for Social Sciences, version 11.5). The classical statistics viz., r, t, ANOVA-F, Levene's-F were utilized on the average score values of indicators of interest. The indicators are psychological health and physical health of the athletes of Manipur at four levels – district, state, national and international. Taking pair combinations with two levels at a time, the components of indicators irrespective of psychological health and physical health of the athletes were analyzed by applying t-test and their significant differences were also examined at 0.05 and 0.01 levels of probability. Besides, the variations in the indications at four different levels were also advocated by utilizing the ANOVA-F. The variations in group variances of the athletes differentiated by four different levels as well as the five different games have also been assessed with the help of Levene's-F Statistics. The interrelationships among the indicators of physical health and psychological health were determined with product moment correlations (r) and differences were measured by t-test thereon.

(a) Analysis of Psychological Health

It is also to compare the various psychological health of

the athletes of Manipur belonging to different games from the four different levels of the study population. The psychological health of the athletes is measured through a standardized test called Eight State Questionnaire [8SQ] developed by Barton, Cattell and Curran. The test mainly covers eight psychological variables viz. anxiety, stress, depression, regression, fatigue, guilt, extraversion and arousal.

Table - 4

Test for variability in psychological health measured by anxiety of athletes at different levels

Level (50 cases each)	*Mean ± S.D*	*Test-values*		
		Level combination	*t-value*	*Levene's-F*
District (D)	14.562.91	D, S	2.237*(0.028)	0.142 (0.707)
State (S)	15.903.07	D, N	4.016**(0.000)	16.650**(0.000)
National (N)	16.401.41	D, I	3.213**(0.002)	3.206 (0.076)
International (I)	16.322.55	S, N	1.045 (0.298)	8.844**(0.004)
		S, I	0.744 (0.459)	1.572 (0.213
		N, I	0.194 (0.847)	2.351(0.128)
All level	15.792.66	ANOVA (F) = 5.491**, P = 0.001		

* *indicates significance at 0.05 level (2-tailed)*
** *indicates significance at 0.01 level (2-tailed)*
Figures in parentheses indicate P-value.

Table-4 depicts the distribution of the average score of psychological health as quantified by anxiety of the athletes at four different levels. It is found the maximum score, 16.40 ± 1.41 at national level followed by international level, 16.32 ± 2.55 and state level, 15.90 ± 3.07 and the minimum score value is at district level. These are deviated from the average score of all levels viz., 15.79 ± 2.66. Here, the level pair combinations consisting of district level are found to have significant variations as advocated by t-values. These are (D,S; t=2.237, P=0.028), (D,N; t=4.016, P=0.000) and (D,I; t=3.213, P=0.002). No statistically significant variations are seen in all pair combinations which are independent of district level despite some visible differences exist thereon. The above significances on the average scores of psychological health status of the athletes under study particularly defined by anxiety may be thought to be caused by the extremely minimum value of district level.

Besides, highly significant difference of group variances are also existed in two pair combinations viz., district and national (Levene's F=16.650, P<0.01) and state and national (Levene's F=8.844, P<0.01) shown in Table 4. However, the average score of anxiety of the athletes in the study population varies, at a glance, highly significantly at four different levels (ANOVA-F=5.4191, P=0.001).

With reference to the above analysis and based on the sten norms porforma, it is found that the anxiety level of the athletes belonging to district level found to be in average while the athletes of state, national and international level lies in slightly deviant i.e above average corresponding to a sten of 7. So, according to this result, it is clear that entering into the higher stages the level of anxiety also increased when compare to initial stage.

The variability in psychological health measured by stress of the athletes under study is depicted in table 5. The findings shows that there is statistically different average scores of stress at four different levels as quantified by the ANOVA (F)-value, 3.669 (P=0.013). The lowest score say 12.482.60 is existed in national level which is deviated from the overall average score 13.432.58 while the maximum value, 14.102.53 falls at state level. Though having visible variations in the scores at four different levels, the significantly different pair combinations associated with that of national level. The combinations are district and national (t=2.183, P<0.05), state and national (t=3.157, P<0.01) and national and international (t=2.105, P<0.05). No statistically different group variances (P>0.05 for Levene's F test) are found in each pair combinations of the athletes in the study population, differentiated by the psychological health status defined by stress.

Table - 5

Test for variability in psychological health measured by stress of athletes at different levels

Level (50 cases each)	*Mean ± S.D*	*Test-values*		
		Level combination	*t-value*	*Levene's-F*
District (D)	13.662.80	D, S	0.823 (0.412)	0.038 (0.845)
State (S)	14.102.53	D, N	2.183*(0.031)	C.071 (0.791)
National (N)	12.482.60	D, I	0.361 (0.719)	0.331 (0.567)
International (I)	13.482.13	S, N	3.157**(0.002)	0.008 (0.931)
		S, I	1.324 (0.188)	0.922 (0.339)
		N, I	2.105*(0.038)	1.059(0.306)
All level	13.432.58	ANOVA (F) = 3.669*, P = 0.013		

* *indicates significance at 0.05 level (2-tailed)*
** *indicates significance at 0.01 level (2-tailed)*
Figures in parentheses indicate P-value.

Utilizing the above information it is now cleared that athletes coming from district, state and international levels has been categorized under an average sten score of 5 for which the interval is from 13 – 15. But in the case of national level the raw score falls in between the 5 and 6 which are both average. So, obviously it can be considered as an average. Despite visible statistical differences all the levels of the study population were in the average while quantified by stress.

Table - 6
Test for variability in psychological health measured by depression of athletes at different levels

Level (50 cases each)	*Mean ± S.D*	*Test-values*		
		Level com-bination	*t-value*	*Levene's-F*
District (D)	14.322.76	D, S	0.464 (0.644)	0.327 (0.569)
State (S)	14.582.84	D, N	3.380**(0.001)	7.376**(0.008)
National (N)	15.841.58	D, I	0.553 (0.581)	3.201 (0.077)
International (I)	14.581.85	S, N	2.738**(0.007)	12.865**(0.001)
		S, I	0.002 (0.978)	6.705*(0.011)
		N, I	3.657**(0.000)	1.641(0.203)
All level	14.832.38	ANOVA (F) = 4.331**, P = 0.006		

** indicates significance at 0.05 level (2-tailed)*
*** indicates significance at 0.01 level (2-tailed)*
Figures in parentheses indicate P-value.

The distribution of the average score of psychological health measured by depression of the athletes differentiated by the four different levels is shown in table 6. As in the case of anxiety, the psychological health status, quantified by depression, of the athletes varies highly significantly at four different levels (F=4.331, P=0.006). While the overall average score of depression is 14.83 ± 2.38, the maximum score (15.84 ± 1.58) is observed at national level and the minimum score (14.32 ± 2.76) is existed at district level in the study population. A similar average score of the health status (depression) is observed at state level (14.58 ± 2.84) and at international level (14.58 ± 1.85) in the study. In this tiny section, the level pair combinations consisting of national level are found have significant variations as evidenced by the classical statistics-t. These are (D,N; t=3.380, P=0.001), (S,N; t=2.738, P=0.007) and (N,I; t=3.657, P=0.000). No statistically significant variations are observed in all pair combinations which are independent of national level despite some visible differences exist thereon. The above significances on the average scores of psychological health (depression) of the athletes may be thought to be caused by the extreme value of national level. Besides, statistically significant differences of group variances are also existed in three pair combinations viz., (D,N; Levene's F=7.376, P=0.008), (S,N; Levene's F=12.865, P=0.001) and (S,I; Levene's F=6.705, P=0.011), depicted in table 6.

By finding that the raw scores of all the four levels lies within the internal 13 – 16 for depression, we see that this corresponds to a sten of 6 which is average. So apart from the negligible value of difference it is concluded that athletes from all there four level seems to be in an almost equal state of depression.

Table-7 also shows the distribution of average score of the psychological health of the athletes particularly defined by regression according to four different levels say district, state, national and international. While the overall average score of the regression is 13.77 ± 2.62, the maximum score, 14.38 ± 2.55 is observed at national level followed by 14.04 ± 3.23 at district level and 13.80 ± 2.13 at national level and the lowest score, 12.86 ± 2.27 at international level. This variation is statistically different at 0.05 probability level of significance as witnessed by test statistics (F=3.192, P=0.025). The significance may be thought to be caused by the extremely low value in the health status (regression) of the athletes at international level.

Table - 7
Test for variability in psychological health measured by regression of athletes at different levels

Level (50 cases each)	*Mean ± S.D*	*Test-values*		
		Level combination	*t-value*	*Levene's-F*
District (D)	14.043.23	D, S	0.584 (0.560)	0.951 (0.332)
State (S)	14.382.55	D, N	0.439 (0.662)	5.064*(0.027)
National (N)	13.802.13	D, I	2.113*(0.037)	4.445*(0.038)
International (I)	12.862.27	S, N	1.236 (0.220)	2.583 (0.111)
		S, I	3.152**(0.002)	2.078 (0.153)
		N, I	2.137*(0.038)	0.003(0.955)
All level	13.772.62	ANOVA (F) = 3.192*, P = 0.025		

** indicates significance at 0.05 level (2-tailed)*
*** indicates significance at 0.01 level (2-tailed)*
Figures in parentheses indicate P-value.

Three pair combinations out of six ones have also found to be significant difference in their psychological health (regression). Each significant combination consists of the athletes of international level. They are district and international (t=2.113, P<0.05), state and international (t=3.152, P<0.01) and national and international (t=2.137, P<0.05). By computing Levene's F only two pair combinations – district and national (5.064, P<0.05) and district and international (4.445, P<0.05) are found to have their significantly different group variances in the study population shown in Table 7.

Like in the case of depression, from the above findings we can see that the psychological health measured by regression at various levels was also found to be statistically different at 0.05 probability level. But apart from this statistical views, the athlete playing at different four levels of the study population were categorized as average as their slightly different raw score lies under the interval 11 – 13 and 14 – 17 corresponding to a sten of 5 and 6 which is observed to be average.

Table - 8

Test for variability in psychological health measured by fatigue of athletes at different levels

Level (50 cases each)	*Mean ± S.D*	*Test-values*		
		Level combination	*t-value*	*Levene's-F*
District (D)	16.242.45	D, S	1.526 (0.130)	0.222 (0.639)
State (S)	17.022.66	D, N	0.334 (0.739)	4.010*(0.048)
National (N)	16.381.68	D, I	0.124 (0.902)	0.078 (0.780)
International (I)	16.302.39	S, N	1.439 (0.153)	5.879*(0.017)
		S, I	1.423 (0.158)	0.055 (0.816)
		N, I	0.194 (0.847)	6.480*(0.012)
All level	16.492.33	ANOVA (F) = 1.208, P = 0.308		

** indicates significance at 0.05 level (2-tailed)*
Figures in parentheses indicate P-value.

As in the case of extraversion, the athletes under study have statistically similar psychological health status quantified by fatigue with respect to four different levels (F=1.208, P>0.05) which is manifested in Table 8. While investigating whether significant differences of the health status (fatigue) in the pair combinations of the athletes exist or not, the findings following classical t-test have illustrated that each pair combination has no statistically differences (P>0.05) thereon. In this analysis, only three pair combinations have their statistically significant difference group variances of the psychological health (fatigue). Utilizing Levene's F test, the significant pair combinations are detected to be district and national (D,N; 4.010, P<0.05), state and national (S,N; 5.879, P<0.05) and national and international (N,I; 6.480, P<0.05).

As depicted by the above findings, the fatigue of athletes at all levels of the study population fall in an interval of 14 – 18 being converted into an average sten score of 6. Further, it can be said that the level of fatigue at the different four levels are categorized in the same condition.

Table - 9

Test for variability in psychological health measured by guilt of athletes at different levels

Level (50 cases each)	*Mean ± S.D*	*Test-values*		
		Level com-bination	*t-value*	*Levene's-F*
District (D)	14.041.87	D, S	2.125*(0.036)	5.892*(0.017)
State (S)	15.002.59	D, N	0.530 (0.597)	1.099 (0.297)
National (N)	14.221.50	D, I	0.102 (0.919)	0.326 (0.570)
International (I)	14.002.05	S, N	1.844 (0.068)	12.761**(0.001)
		S, I	2.142*(0.035)	3.380 (0.069)
		N, I	0.612 (0.542)	2.669(0.106)
All level	14.322.07	ANOVA (F) = 2.613, P = 0.053		

** indicates significance at 0.05 level (2-tailed)*
*** indicates significance at 0.01 level (2-tailed).*
Figures in parentheses indicate P-value.

In the case of psychological health status defined by guilt, the average score values are distributed according to four levels in table 9. While the score for all athletes is found to be 14.32 ± 2.07, the visible differences at the four levels are 14.04 ± 1.87 (district), 15.002.59 (state), 14.22 ± 1.50 (national) and 14.00 ± 2.05 (international). These variations are found to be not different statistically at four levels as evidenced by F-value, 2.613 (P>0.05). It emphasizes that there is no difference in the psychological health of the athletes in the study population particularly defined by guilt. Only two level pair combinations viz., (D,S; t=2.125, P<0.05) and (S,I; t=2.142, P<0.05) have significant differences in the psychological health (guilt) of the athletes. Also only two pair combinations say district and state (P<0.05) and state and national (P<0.01) have statistically been found to be significant difference at their group variances in the analysis, depicted in Table 9.

So, as given by the sten norms, raw scores of all the four levels come within the interval 12–16 for guilt, occupying a sten of 7 which is slightly deviant of above average. This further concludes that no dough these small population falls higher than the average but there is almost an equal psychological health status as given by guilt for all the athletes hailing from different levels.

Table - 10
Test for variability in psychological health measured by extraversion of athletes at different levels

Level (50 cases each)	*Mean ± S.D*	*Test-values*		
		Level combination	*t-value*	*Levene's-F*
District (D)	16.283.00	D, S	1.617 (0.109)	2.398 (0.125)
State (S)	17.363.65	D, N	0.825 (0.411)	6.821*(0.011)
National (N)	16.701.99	D, I	0.552 (0.582)	0.427 (0.515)
International	15.962.80	S, N	1.122 (0.265)	17.015**(0.000)
(I)		S, I	2.151*(0.034)	4.661*(0.033)
		N, I	1.523 (0.131)	3.439(0.067)
All level	16.582.95	ANOVA (F) = 2.143, P = 0.096		

* *indicates significance at 0.05 level (2-tailed)*
** *indicates significance at 0.01 level (2-tailed)*
Figures in parentheses indicate P-value.

There is no statistically significant variation of psychological health status specifically defined by extraversion of the athletes according to four different levels– district, state, national and international in the study population. It is witnessed by the F-value, 2.143 (P=0.096) despite some visible difference exist in the average scores at the four levels shown in table 10. Besides, all the pair level combinations except one, (S,I; t=2.151, P<0.05), are also found statistically insignificant differences in psychological health status measured by extraversion. However, three pair level combinations have statistically significant group variances in their psychological health (extraversion). Being quantified by Levene's-F, the significant combinations are district and national (6.821, P<0.05), state and national (17.015, P<0.01) and state and international (4.661, P<0.05).

Taking into consideration of the above findings, it is seen that the athletes belonging to district, state and national levels fall under the average sten of 5. Also athlete for international level has gross score of 15.96 which is very much near to 16 so it is also taken to have average sten score of 5. So, it may now conclude that athletes according to four levels are almost average in psychological health specially measured by extraversion.

The variation in psychological health measured by arousal of the athletes at different levels is furnished in Table 11. While the average score value of all the athletes differentiated by four different levels is 14.24 ± 2.39, then the maximum score, 15.34 ± 2.75 is observed at state level and the minimum score value, 13.72 ± 1.95 is existed at national level. In this analysis, the average score o psychological health status (arousal) of the athletes is found to vary at four levels – district, state, national and international. This variation is highly significant at 0.01 probability level as witnessed by F-value, 5.155 (P=0.002). By utilizing the classical t-statistics, three level pair combinations say (D,S; t=2.896, P=0.005),

(S,N; t=3.397, P=0.001) and (S,I; t=2.665, P=0.000) are observed to be significantly different at 0.01 level of significance. It may be noted that each significant combination consists of state level owing to its extreme score value at an average, 15.34 ± 2.75. However, no group variances among the four different levels are found statistically different (Levene's F-test with P>0.05).

Table – 11

Test for variability in psychological health measured by arousal of athletes at different levels

Level (50 cases each)	*Mean ± S.D*	*Test-values*		
		Level combination	*t-value*	*Levene's-F*
District (D)	13.882.26	D, S	2.896**(0.005)	2.925 (0.090)
State (S)	15.342.75	D, N	0.379 (0.706)	0.001 (0.981)
National (N)	13.721.95	D, I	0.266 (0.791)	0.174 (0.677)
International	14.002.25	S, N	3.397**(0.001)	3.818 (0.054)
(I)		S, I	2.665**(0.000)	1.933 (0.168)
		N, I	0.665 (0.507)	0.223(0.638)
All level	14.242.39	ANOVA (F) = 5.155**, P = 0.002		

** indicates significance at 0.05 level (2-tailed)*
*** indicates significance at 0.01 level (2-tailed)*
Figures in parentheses indicate P-value.

From the above finding, it is seen that the mean row scores of all the levels say district, state, national and international were found to be statistically varied. But in contradiction to this result while referring to sten norms porforma of study manual, their raw scores falls under the interval of 13 – 16 occupying a sten of 4 with is slightly deviant which is below the average. So, it can be summarized that athletes belonging to these four levels occupies a category of low arousal status.

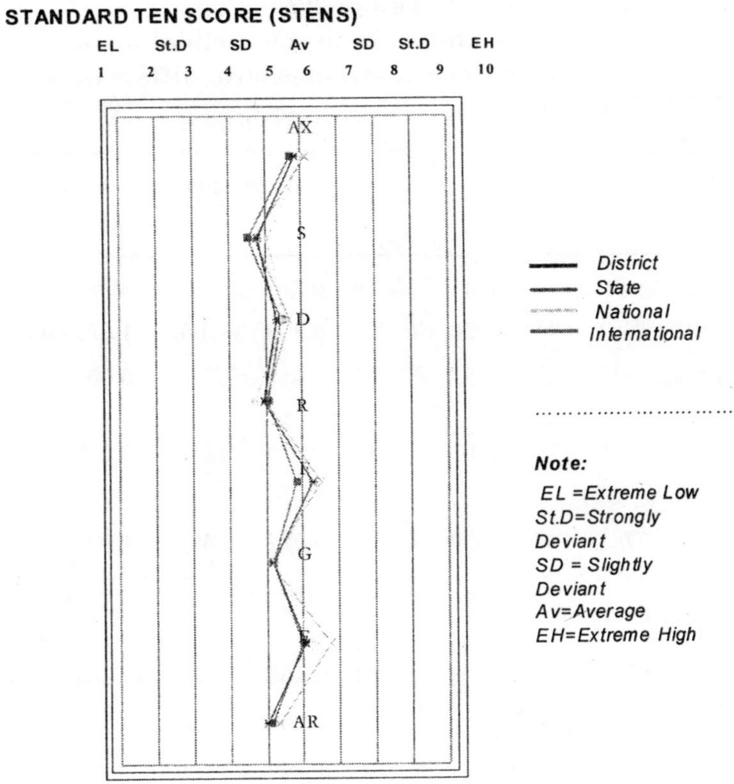

Fig.1: Variation in Psychological Health of the Athlete at Different Levels

Anxiety (Ax): Worried, easily rattled, tense, emotionally upset, easily angered, high strung, easily annoyed.**Stress (S):** Feeing a lot of pressure, unable to take time off and relax, constantly on the go, great strain, unhappy with own performance, experiencing lots of demand.**Depression (D):** Unhappy, disagreeable, pessimistic in poor spirit, disappointed.**Regression (R):** Confused, unorganized, unable to concentrate, experiencing difficulty coping, acting impulsively..**Fatigue (F):** Exhausted, no energy, sluggish, tired, needing rest, weary, below par in performance.**Guilt (G):** Regretful, concern about own misdeeds, experiencing difficulties, sleeping unkind, dissatisfied with self.**Extraversion (E):** Sociable, outgoing, talkative, enthusiastic.**Arousal (A):** Alert, keyed up, excited, stimulated, keen and sharp

Table – 12
Test for variability in psychological health measured by anxiety of athletes with different items

Level (40 cases each)	*Mean ± S.D*	*Test-values*		
		Game combination	*t-value*	*Levene's-F*
Fencing (FC)	15.582.11	FC, SR	0.285 (0.777)	9.403**(0.002)
Soccer (SR)	15.403.26	FC, TK	0.809 (0.421)	1.622 (0.207)
Taekwondo (TK)	16.103.52	FC, ST	1.412 (0.162)	0.001 (0.984)
Sepak-Takraw (ST)	16.232.01	FC, JD	0.218 (0.828)	0.230 (0.633)
Judo (JD)	15.681.99	SR, TK	0.922 (0.359)	1.034 (0.312)
		SR, ST	1.362 (0.177)	10.713**(0.002)
		SR, JD	0.455 (0.651)	9.303**(0.003)
		TK, ST	0.195 (0.846)	1.666 (0.201)
		TK, JD	0.664 (0.508)	1.092 (0.299)
		ST, JD	1.230 (0.222)	0.242(0.624)
All items	15.792.66	ANOVA (F) = 0.700, P = 0.593		

** indicates significance at 0.05 level (2-tailed)*
*** indicates significance at 0.01 level (2-tailed)*
Figures in parentheses indicate P-value.

The variability in the psychological health quantified by anxiety of the athletes is furnished in Table 12 with respect to five different items under study. Though having some visible variations, the average scores of anxiety of the athletes vary insignificantly with five different items (F=0.700, P>0.05). Each ten pair combinations of the athletes differentiated by items also found statistically not different in their psychological health status (anxiety) as advocated by the insignificant classical t-values (P>0.05). Only three combinations – (FC,SR), (SR,ST) and (SR,JD) out of its ten are highly significantly different in their respective variances at 0.01 probability level (Table 12).

As been highlighted in the above findings, the raw scores for all the items fall in the interval 15 – 18 corresponding to a sten of 7 which is slightly deviant. Hence, the athletes playing all the five different games are almost equal in their psychological health status as measured by anxiety.

Table - 13

Test for variability in psychological health measured by stress of athletes with different items

Level (40 cases each)	*Mean ± S.D*	*Test-values*		
		Game combination	*t-value*	*Levene's-F*
Fencing (FC)	12.932.55	FC, SR	0.216 (0.830)	0.117 (0.734)
Soccer (SR)	13.052.64	FC, TK	2.182*(0.032)	0.091 (0.764)
Taekwondo (TK)	14.152.48	FC, ST	0.966 (0.337)	0.073 (0.788)
Sepak-Takraw (ST)	13.452.31	FC, JD	1.079 (0.284)	0.795 (0.375)
Judo (JD)	13.582.84	SR, TK	1.922 (0.058)	0.004 (0.950)
		SR, ST	0.721 (0.473)	0.015 (0.903)
		SR, JD	0.857 (0.394)	1.336 (0.251)
		TK, ST	1.308 (0.195)	0.004 (0.953)
		TK, JD	0.966 (0.337)	1.400 (0.240)
		ST, JD	0.216 (0.829)	1.518 (0.222)
All items	13.432.58	ANOVA (F) = 1.425, P = 0.227		

** indicates significance at 0.05 level (2-tailed)*

Figures in parentheses indicate P-value.

In Table-13 the average scores of stress as a measure of psychological health of the athletes are independently and identically distributed according to five different games. The average scores corresponding to different games deviated insignificantly (F=1.425, P=0.227) from their overall mean score viz., 13.43 ± 2.58. It scientifically means that the average scores of stress of the athletes are statistically similar according to five different games – fencing (12.93 ± 2.55), soccer (13.05 ± 2.64), taekwondo (14.15 ± 2.48), sepak-takraw (13.45 ± 2.31) and judo (13.58 ± 2.84). Thus, the five different games can not differentiate the level of psychological health in its stress of the athletes in the study population. There is no significant difference between two items in its average scores of stress on the athletes for all pair combinations except one viz., (FC,TK; P<0.05) shown in table 13.Utilizing Levene's F-test, all pair combinations have also found to be insignificant variations in their group variances (P>0.05).

Above findings reveal that the raw scores fall under the same interval of 13 – 15 except in the case of fencing where the raw score 12.93 falls between sten 4 and 5. But 12.93 is very much near 13 it can be considered to be in the interval of 13 – 15 which corresponds to a average sten of 5. Hence, it can be concluded that altogether all the athletes pertaining to all the five difference games belong to the same sten of 5 which is average.

The average scores of depression as a measure of psychological health of the athletes are independently and identically distributed according to five different games, shown in Table 14. The average scores corresponding to different games cannot be deviated significantly (F=0.975, P>0.05) from their overall mean score viz., 14.83 ± 2.38. It scientifically means that the average scores of depression of the athletes under study are statistically similar according to five different games – fencing (14.35 ± 2.36), soccer (14.90 ± 3.17), taekwondo (14.98 $\pm$ 2.34), sepak- takraw (15.33 $\pm$ 1.83) and judo (14.60 $\pm$ 2.00). Thus, the five different games can not differentiate the level of psychological health in its depression of the athletes in the study population.

Table - 14

Test for variability in psychological health measured by depression of athletes with different items

Level (40 cases each)	*Mean ± S.D*	*Test-values*		
		Game com-bination	*t-value*	*Levene's-F*
Fencing (FC)	14.352.36	FC, SR	0.880 (0.381)	0.001 (0.980)
Soccer (SR)	14.903.17	FC, TK	1.190 (0.238)	0.685 (0.410)
Taekwondo (TK)	14.982.34	FC, ST	2.065*(0.042)	8.111**(0.008)
Sepak-Takraw (ST)	15.331.83	FC, JD	0.511 (0.610)	4.153*(0.045)
Judo (JD)	14.602.00	SR, TK	0.120 (0.904)	0.244 (0.623)
		SR, ST	0.734 (0.465)	2.707 (0.104)
		SR, JD	0.507 (0.614)	1.387 (0.243)
		TK, ST	0.746 (0.458)	2.790 (0.099)
		TK, JD	0.771 (0.443)	0.960 (0.330)
		ST, JD	1.692 (0.095)	0.552(0.460)
All items	14.832.38	ANOVA (F) = 0.975, P = 0.422		

** indicates significance at 0.05 level (2-tailed)*
*** indicates significance at 0.01 level (2-tailed)*
Figures in parentheses indicate P-value.

There is no significant difference between two items in its average scores of depression of the athletes for all pair combinations except one, (FC,ST; P<0.05) shown in Table

14. Utilizing Levene's F-test, eight out of ten pair combinations have also insignificant group variances (P>0.05). The significant two pairs are (FC,ST; 8.111, P<0.01) and (FC,JD; 4.153, P<0.05).

It is now observed that there is not much differences for depression in relation to the above mentioned five games as the raw score are all included in the interval 13 – 16 relating to a sten of 6. This clearly indicates that athletes belonging to all these five games are in the average status for depression.

Table – 15

Test for variability in psychological health measured by regression of athletes with different items

Level (40 cases each)	*Mean ± S.D*	*Test-values*		
		Game combination	*t-value*	*Levene's-F*
Fencing (FC)	13.552.22	FC, SR	0.912 (0.364)	2.871 (0.094)
Soccer (SR)	14.082.89	FC, TK	0.328 (0.744)	0.385 (0.537)
Taekwondo (TK)	13.382.55	FC, ST	0.780 (0.438)	1.828 (0.180)
Sepak-Takraw (ST)	13.982.64	FC, JD	0.572 (0.569)	1.249 (0.267)
Judo (JD)	13.882.83	SR, TK	1.150 (0.254)	1.019 (0.316)
		SR, ST	0.162 (0.872)	0.181 (0.672)
		SR, JD	0.313 (0.755)	0.210 (0.648)
		TK, ST	1.035 (0.304)	0.412 (0.523)
		TK, JD	0.830 (0.409)	0.253 (0.617)
		ST, JD	0.164 (0.871)	0.006 (0.938)
All items	13.772.62	ANOVA (F) = 0.505, P = 0.732		

Figures in parentheses indicate P-value.

Though there are some visible variations in the scores of psychological health measured by regression of the athletes differentiated by five different games, they cannot be significant statistically therein ($F=0.505$, $P>0.05$). The finding indicates that the scores of regression of the athletes cannot be differentiated significantly in the study population (table 15). Taking the two groups of athletes according to five different games at a time (pair combination), we have no statistically difference ($P>0.05$) in each ten pairs as witnessed by the insignificant values of classical t-test. These pair combinations of the athletes with types of games have also similar group variances ($P>0.05$) in the study by applying Levene's F-test.

Thus, it can be interpreted that raw scores of athletes from games like fencing, taekwondo, sepak-takraw and judo falls between sten of 5 and 6 both of which are average. As a result it can be concluded that these said games falls in the category of average. Besides raw scores of athletes playing soccer lies in the interval 14 – 17 thus obtaining a sten of 6 which is also average. Finally, as a whole it can be summarized those athletes from all the five different games fall in the category of average.

No significant differences on average scores of psychological health defined by fatigue of the athletes are detected according to different items ($F=1.998$, $P=0.096$) shown in Table 16. It emphasizes that the scores of the extraversion of the athletes are similarly existed with five items say fencing (16.52 ± 1.97), soccer (15.63 ± 2.75), taekwondo (16.70 ± 2.57), sepak-takraw (17.00 ± 1.85) and judo (16.58 ± 2.24). Nine pair combinations except one of the athletes with their different items are found to be insignificant difference ($P>0.05$) in their scores of fatigue. The lone significant pair is (SR,ST; $t=2.621$, $P<0.05$).

Table – 16

Test for variability in psychological health measured by fatigue of athletes with different items

Level (40 cases each)	*Mean ± S.D*	*Test-values*		
		Game combination	*t-value*	*Levene's-F*
Fencing (FC)	16.521.97	FC, SR	1.681 (0.097)	2.167 (0.145)
Soccer (SR)	15.632.75	FC, TK	0.341 (0.734)	0.744 (0.391)
Taekwondo (TK)	16.702.57	FC, ST	1.109 (0.271)	0.662 (0.418)
Sepak-Takraw (ST)	17.001.85	FC, JD	0.106 (0.916)	0.008 (0.927)
Judo (JD)	16.582.24	SR, TK	1.804 (0.075)	0.272 (0.604)
		SR, ST	2.621*(0.011)	4.210*(0.044)
		SR, JD	1.693 (0.094)	1.541 (0.218)
		TK, ST	0.598 (0.551)	2.142 (0.147)
		TK, JD	0.232 (0.817)	0.481 (0.490)
		ST, JD	0.924 (0.358)	0.592(0.444)
All items	16.492.33	ANOVA (F) = 1.998, P = 0.096		

** indicates significance at 0.05 level (2-tailed)*
Figures in parentheses indicate P-value.

With reference to the above results, the raw scores for all the respective five games are included within the interval 14 – 18 representing an average sten of 6. As a result, athlete practicing these five games has got somewhat similar responses for fatigue.

Table – 17
Test for variability in psychological health measured by guilt of athletes with different items

Level (40 cases each)	*Mean ± S.D*	*Test-values*		
		Game combination	*t-value*	*Levene's-F*
Fencing (FC)	14.132.08	FC, SR	0.524 (0.602)	0.038 (0.846)
Soccer (SR)	14.382.19	FC, TK	0.852 (0.397)	0.844 (0.361)
Taekwondo (TK)	14.501.85	FC, ST	0.283 (0.778)	1.162 (0.284)
Sepak-Takraw (ST)	14.251.86	FC, JD	0.400 (0.690)	0.706 (0.403)
Judo (JD)	14.332.38	SR, TK	0.275 (0.784)	0.381 (0.539)
		SR, ST	0.275 (0.784)	0.595 (0.443)
		SR, JD	0.098 (0.922)	0.891 (0.348)
		TK, ST	0.601 (0.549)	0.039 (0.845)
		TK, JD	0.367 (0.715)	2.898 (0.093)
		ST, JD	0.157 (0.876)	3.345 (0.071)
All items	14.322.07	ANOVA (F) = 0.180, P = 0.948		

Figures in parentheses indicate P-value.

As in case of fatigue, there is also insignificant differences on average scores of psychological health quantified by guilt of the athletes differentiated by five different items (F=0.180, P=0.948) which is manifested in table 17. It again shows that the scores of guilt of the athletes are similarly existed with five items say fencing (14.13 ± 2.08), soccer (14.38 ± 2.19), taekwondo (14.501.85), sepak-takraw (14.25 ± 1.86) and judo (14.33 ± 2.38). All pair combinations of the athletes with their different items are found to be insignificant difference (P>0.05) in the scores of guilt. No significant group variances of each pair combination are also found in the analysis.

As per the above findings, the raw score of guilt of the athlete exists in the interval 12 – 16 leading to a sten of 7 which is slightly deviant. It is thus being concluded that similar cases of slightly deviant are found for all the five different items.

Table – 18
Test for variability in psychological health measured by extraversion of athletes with different items

Level (40 cases each)	*Mean ± S.D*	*Test-values*		
		Game combination	*t-value*	*Levene's-F*
Fencing (FC)	16.702.32	FC, SR	1.187 (0.239)	3.576 (0.062)
Soccer (SR)	15.953.25	FC, TK	0.080 (0.937)	1.302 (0.257)
Taekwondo (TK)	16.653.21	FC, ST	1.451 (0.151)	1.027 (0.314)
Sepak-Takraw (ST)	17.502.60	FC, JD	1.019 (0.311)	2.141 (0.147)
Judo (JD)	16.083.11	SR, TK	0.968 (0.336)	0.285 (0.595)
		SR, ST	2.355* (0.021)	1.097 (0.298)
		SR, JD	0.176 (0.861)	0.144 (0.706)
		TK, ST	1.300 (0.197)	0.134 (0.715)
		TK, JD	0.813 (0.419)	0.032 (0.858)
		ST, JD	2.223*(0.029)	0.382(0.538)
All items	16.582.95	ANOVA (F) = 1.776, P = 0.135		

** indicates significance at 0.05 level (2-tailed)*
Figures in parentheses indicate P-value.

Table 18 illustrates the distribution of average scores of the extraversion as a measure of psychological health of the athletes according to five different games under study. While the overall average scores of extraversion of the athletes is (162.95), the highest score (17.50 ± 2.60) is found in sepak-takraw and the lowest one (15.95 ± 3.25) is existed in soccer. The scores of other games – fencing, taekwondo, and judo are also deviated a little from the overall average score. Notwithstanding, the score value of extraversion of the athletes varies insignificantly with five different games in the study population (F=1.776, P=0.135). Only two out of ten pair combinations say (SC,ST; t=2.355, P=0.021) and (ST,JD; t=2.223, P=0.029) are found significant in their average scores of extraversion at only 0.05 probability level. No statistically significant (Levene's F-test, P>0.05) group variances are also found for all pair combinations of the athletes with respect to different items.

Falling the above illustration it is quite clear that athletes playing fencing, taekwondo, sepak-takraw and judo are altogether categorized in an average sten of 5. For those playing soccer the raw score is 15.95 which is very much near to 16 and hence it is also taken as an average of 5.

Table – 19
Test for variability in psychological health measured by arousal of athletes with different items

Level (40 cases each)	*Mean ± S.D*	*Test-values*		
		Game combination	*t-value*	*Levene's-F*
Fencing (FC)	13.551.58	FC, SR	1.142 (0.257)	18.183**(0.000)
Soccer (SR)	14.303.84	FC, TK	2.541*(0.013)	4.697*(0.033)
Taekwondo (TK)	14.632.16	FC, ST	2.721**(0.008)	1.117 (0.294)
Sepak-Takraw (ST)	14.652.01	FC, JD	1.419 (0.160)	0.085 (0.772)
Judo (JD)	14.051.57	SR, TK	0.467 (0.642)	8.380**(0.005)
		SR, ST	0.511 (0.186)	11.717**(0.001)
		SR, JD	0.381 (0.704)	19.137**(0.000)
		TK, ST	0.054 (0.957)	0.811 (0.371)
		TK, JD	1.364 (0.177)	5.590*(0.021)
		ST, JD	1.490 (0.140)	1.617(0.207)
All items	14.242.39	ANOVA (F) = 1.466, P = 0.214		

** indicates significance at 0.05 level (2-tailed)*
*** indicates significance at 0.01 level (2-tailed)*
Figures in parentheses indicate P-value.

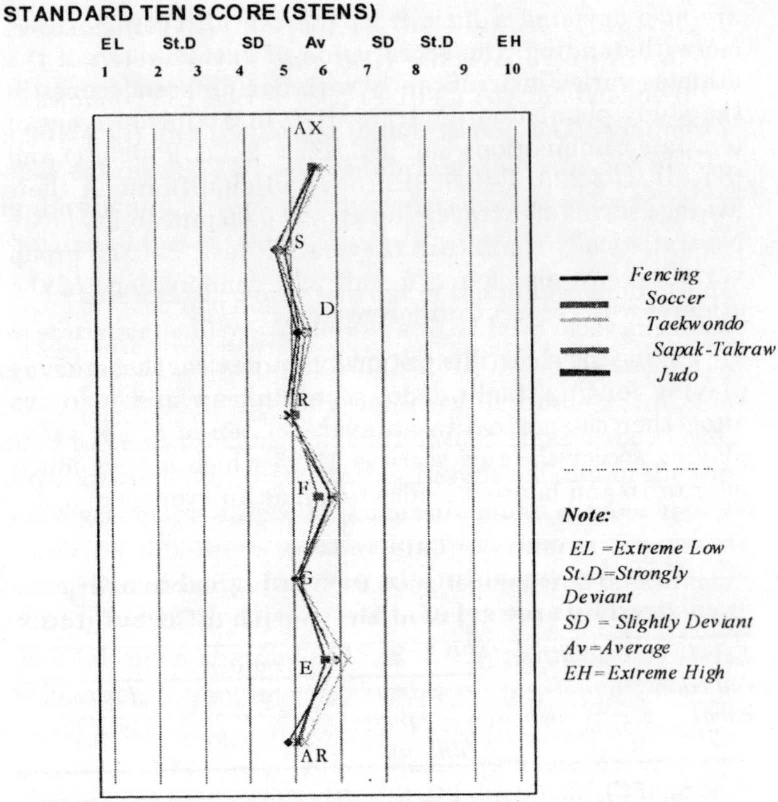

Fig.2: Variation in Psychological Health of the Athlete at Different Games

Anxiety (Ax): Worried, easily rattled, tense, emotionally upset, easily angered, high strung, easily annoyed.**Stress (S):** Feeing a lot of pressure, unable to take time off and relax, constantly on the go, great strain, unhappy with own performance, experiencing lots of demand.**Depression (D):** Unhappy, disagreeable, pessimistic in poor spirit, disappointed.**Regression (R):** Confused, unorganized, unable to concentrate, experiencing difficulty coping, acting impulsively. **Fatigue (F):** Exhausted, no energy, sluggish, tired, needing rest, weary, below par in performance.**Guilt (G):** Regretful, concern about own misdeeds, experiencing difficulties, sleeping unkind, dissatisfied with self.**Extraversion (E):** Sociable, outgoing, talkative, enthusiastic.**Arousal (A):** Alert, keyed up, excited, stimulated, keen and sharp

No statistical difference is found in the psychological health status defined by arousal of the athletes differentiated with five different items – fencing (FC), soccer (SR), taekwondo (TK), sepak-takraw (ST) and judo (JD) as witnessed by the value of F-statistics, 1.466 (P>0.05) which is depicted in table 19. Despite, some visible differences exist in the mean scores of arousal among the athletes of five different games.

Utilizing the classical t-test on the ten pair combinations of athletes according to the five different items, we have only two combinations are found significantly different. The pair combinations of the athletes are of (FC, TK; 2.541, P<0.05) and (FC, ST; 2.721, P<0.01). It indicates that almost pair combinations of athletes differentiated by five items have similarly distributed in their psychological health status particularly defined by arousal. However, six pairs of athletes with different items under study have their statistically different group variances as evidenced by Levene's F-test. The significant games are noted to be fencing and soccer (18.183, P<0.01), fencing and taekwondo (4.697, P<0.05), soccer and taekwondo (8.380, P<0.01), soccer and sepak-takraw (11.717, P<0.01), soccer and judo (19.137, P<0.01) and taekwondo and judo (5.590, P<0.05). In this analysis, each pair combination of athletes having highly significant group variances consists the item soccer.

Hence, the quantum of psychological health status as defined by arousal is found to be in the slightly deviant which means lower than the average with a sten score of 4 for all the different five games. As a result, there is not much variations in the psychological health status as defined by arousal for all the above mentioned games. Like in case of game-wise, here also the athletes of the above mentioned games have low level of arousal.

(b) Analysis of Physical Health

It is to compare the physical fitness or health of the

athletes at various level – district, state, national and international players. The level of physical health is quantified by a standardized test called AAHPER Youth Fitness Test consisting of six different items to measure different components say muscular strength, strength endurance, explosive strength, agility, speed, cardio respiratory endurance. Besides height and weight as an additional component for the context of the study.

Table – 20

Test for variability in physical health measured by muscular strength of athletes at different levels

Level (50 cases each)	*Mean ± S.D*	*Test-values*		
		Level com-bination	*t-value*	*Levene's-F*
District (D)	9.993.32	D, S	2.803**(0.006)	2.446 (0.121)
State (S)	12.094.11	D, N	5.737**(0.000)	16.123**(0.000)
National (N)	15.425.82	D, I	10.660**(0.000)	16.163**(0.000)
International (I)	22.537.62	S, N	3.313**(0.001)	6.685* (0.011)
		S, I	8.522**(0.000)	9.187**(0.003)
		N, I	5.238**(0.000)	1.163(0.284)
All level	15.017.23	ANOVA (F) = 50.279**, P = 0.000		

** indicates significance at 0.05 level (2-tailed)*
*** indicates significance at 0.01 level (2-tailed)*
Figures in parentheses indicate P-value.

The variability in physical health measured by pull-ups for muscular strength of the athletes at different levels is manifested in table 20 (Fig.3). The muscular strength of athletes is observed at an average of 15.01 with standard deviation (S. D), 7.23. While the highest value – 22.537.62 found in international level followed by 15.425.82 in national level the lowest value, 9.993.32 is found in district level. The variations are statistically and significantly different at 0.01 probability level as evidenced by ANOVA (F)-value, 50.279 (P=0.000). In this analysis, all the level combinations are statistically as well as highly different at 0.01 level of significance as evidenced by t-values – 2.803 (D,S), 5.737 (D,N), 10.660 (D,I), 3.313 (S,N), 8.522 (S,I) and 5.238 (N,I) shown in table 22. By computing Levene's F, out of the six level combinations, three ones are found to have highly significant difference in their group variances. They are district and national (16.123, P=0.000), district and international (16.163, P=0.000) and state and international (9.187, P=0.003). Another one combination, state and national is also found different at 0.05 probability level (6.685, P=0.011). Thus it may be concluded that the physical health status, defined by muscular strength, of the athletes in study population varies highly at four levels say district, state, national and international.

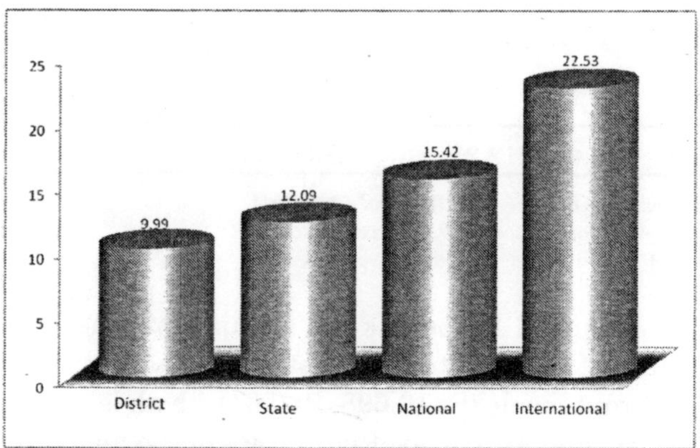

Fig. 3: Variability in Physical Health Measured by Muscular Strength of Athletes at Different Levels (Number of Pull-Up)

Further, from the above findings it is again interpreted that the athletes belonging to state, national and international levels were found to be excellent as their pull-up repetition lies within and above 15. Whereas, the athletes from district level alone falls under the ranking of good having their repetition within 10.

Table – 21

Test for variability in physical health measured by strength endurance of athletes at different levels

Level (50 cases each)	*Mean ± S.D*	*Test-values*		
		Level combination	*t-value*	*Levene's-F*
District (D)	39.4812.40	D, S	4.013**(0.000)	0.033 (0.857)
State (S)	48.9611.19	D, N	4.554**(0.000)	0.350 (0.556)
National (N)	49.8210.20	D, I	6.746**(0.000)	1.591 (0.210)
International (I)	54.649.94	S, N	0.401 (0.689)	0.206 (0.651)
		S, I	2.683**(0.009)	1.453 (0.231)
		N, I	2.392*(0.019)	0.687(0.409)
All level	48.2212.21	ANOVA (F) = 16.698**, P = 0.000		

* *indicates significance at 0.05 level (2-tailed)*
** *indicates significance at 0.01 level (2-tailed)*
Figures in parentheses indicate P-value.

As measured by bent-knee sit-up test, the strength endurance of the athletes under study varies statistically at four different levels (F=16.698, P<0.01) which is manifested in table 21 (Fig. 4). The average values of the measurement are existed in descending order say international (54.64 ± 9.94), national (49.82 ± 10.20), state (48.961 ± 1.19) and district (39.48 ± 12.40). Four pair combinations – district and state, district and national, district and international and state and international are found highly different (P<0.01) in their physical health status measured by strength endurance and one combination say national and international also found statistically different (P<0.05). However, the group variances of all the pair combinations are statistically similarly situated (P>0.05).

Further, it can be concluded that the athletes from district level belongs to a repetition of within 46 stating it as an average ranking. Likewise, athletes from state and national levels belong to a ranking of good as their repetition falls within 52. Lastly, athletes at the international level are found to be excellent in their ranking having a repetition of within 62.

Table – 22

Test for variability in physical health measured by explosive strength of athletes at different levels

Level (50 cases each)	*Mean ± S.D*	*Test-values*		
		Level combination	*t-value*	*Levene's-F*
District (D)	2.000.31	D, S	2.548*(0.012)	2.107 (0.150)
State (S)	2.150.26	D, N	2.177*(0.032)	0.786 (0.377)
National (N)	2.130.28	D, I	5.483**(0.000)	0.014 (0.907)
International (I)	2.360.38	S, N	0.311 (0.756)	0.278 (0.599)
		S, I	3.445**(0.001)	1.850 (0.177)
		N, I	3.616**(0.000)	0.780(0.379)
All level	2.160.32	ANOVA (F) = 11.996**, P = 0.000		

** indicates significance at 0.05 level (2-tailed)*
*** indicates significance at 0.01 level (2-tailed)*
Figures in parentheses indicate P-value.

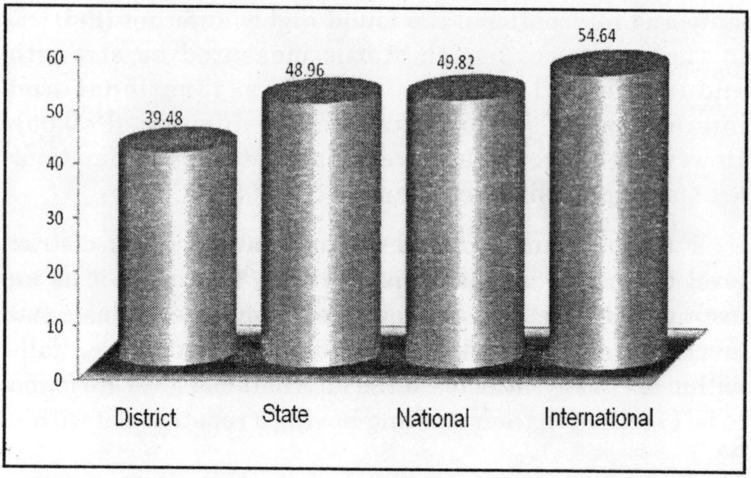

Fig. 4: Variability in Physical Health Measured by Strength Endurance of Athletes at Different Levels (Number of Sit-Up per Minute)

The average score of explosive strength, quantified by standing broad jump, of the athletes for all levels in the study population is found to be 2.16$\pm$0.32. While the maximum score, 2.360.38 is observed at international level followed by state level, 2.150.26 and national level 2.130.28, the minimum score is found to be 2.000.31 at district level. This visible variation is highly and statistically significant at 0.01 probability level as witnessed by F-value, 11.996 (P=0.000), shown in table 22 (Fig. 5).

Out of six level pair combinations three ones are noted highly significantly different at 0.01 probability level. They are district and national (t=2.763, P=0.007), district and international (t=6.732, P=0.000) and state and international (t=4.637, P=0.000). And two combinations say district and state (t=2.548, P=0.012) and district and national (t=2.177, P= 0.32) are also found significantly different at 0.05

probability level. Only three level pair combinations viz., district and state (Levene's F=8.282), state and international (Levene's F=23.345) and national and international (Levene's F=8.848) have their highly significant (P<0.01) group variances in the present analysis.

With reference to the above finding, it is also observed that the mean score of the athletes at international level falls under the distance of 2.36 meters which is meant to be in the ranking of good. On the other hand, the rest of the levels say district, state and national were found to be average in their ranking occupying a distance within 2.18 meters.

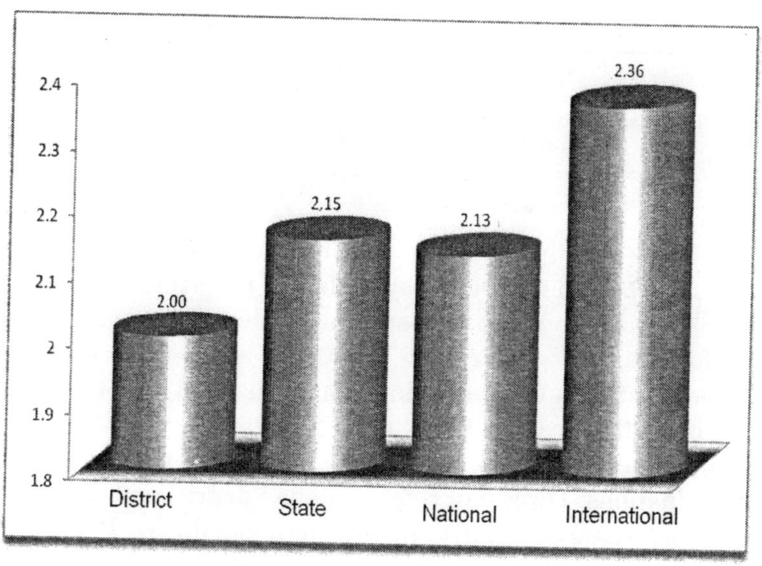

Fig.5: Variability in Physical Health Measured by Explosive Strength of Athletes at Different Levels (In Meters)

Table - 23
Test for variability in physical health measured by agility of athletes at different levels

Level (50 cases each)	*Mean ± S.D*	*Test-values*		
		Level combination	*t-value*	*Levene's-F*
District (D)	9.570.69	D, S	0.778 (0.413)	8.282** (0.005)
State (S)	9.440.94	D, N	2.763**(0.007)	2.662 (0.106)
National (N)	9.100.98	D, I	6.732**(0.000)	3.731 (0.056)
International (I)	8.730.54	S, N	1.779 (0.078)	0.352 (0.554)
		S, I	4.637**(0.000)	23.345**(0.000)
		N, I	2.320*(0.022)	8.848**(0.004)
All level	9.210.87	ANOVA (F) = 10.799**, P = 0.000		

** indicates significance at 0.05 level (2-tailed)*
*** indicates significance at 0.01 level (2-tailed)*
Figures in parentheses indicate P-value.

Table-23 (Fig. 6) shows that the average scores of the physical health measured by agility of the athletes at four levels. It is found that the ascending order of average scores at four levels – district (9.57 ± 0.69), state (9.44 ± 0.94), national (9.10 ± 0.98) and international (8.73 ± 0.54) while the overall average is 9.21 ± 0.87. For statistical analysis, t-test is again applied to check the variations in the level pair combinations. Three pair combinations – district and national (2.763, P=0.007), district and international (6.732, P=0.000) and state and international (4.637, P=0.000) are observed to be highly significant in the analysis. Also national and international players are significantly different (2.320, P=0.022) in their physical health with particular reference to agility in the study population.

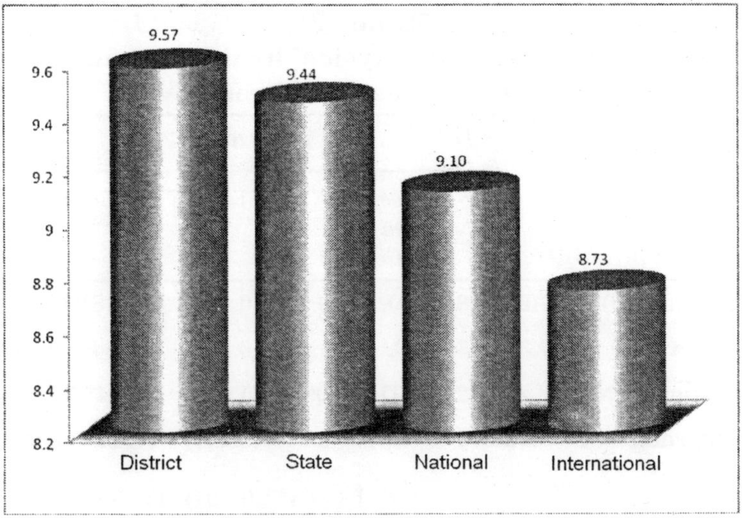

Fig. 6: Variability in Physical Health Measured by Agility of Athletes at Different Levels (In Seconds)

Besides, the three pair combinations viz., district and state, state and international and national and international have their highly significant group variations each at 0.01 probability level. It may worthwhile be concluded that the average score of physical health status quantified by agility varies highly significantly (F=10.799, P=0.000) at four different levels – district, state, national and international.

Looking forward, it can be interprete4d again that athletes belonging to district and state levels are categorized as having good agility as indicated by 10m shuttle run test with their mean score in second falls within 9.7 – 9.2 second whereas it is found to be excellent in the case of national and international level as their performance to complete the course shows before 9.1 – 8.6 seconds.

Table - 24
Test for variability in physical health measured by speed of athletes at different levels

Level (50 cases each)	*Mean ± S.D*	*Test-values*		
		Level combination	*t-value*	*Levene's-F*
District (D)	7.511.18	D, S	0.747 (0.457)	1.481 (0.227)
State (S)	7.341.13	D, N	1.087 (0.279)	0.846 (0.360)
National (N)	7.280.92	D, I	4.093**(0.000)	9.244**(0.003)
International (I)	6.720.70	S, N	0.279 (0.781)	8.516**(0.004)
		S, I	3.304**(0.001)	35.185**(0.000)
		N, I	3.445**(0.001)	7.610**(0.007)
All level	7.211.03	ANOVA (F) = 5.901**, P = 0.001		

** indicates significance at 0.05 level (2-tailed)*
*** indicates significance at 0.01 level (2-tailed)*
Figures in parentheses indicate P-value.

The distribution of physical health status quantified by speed of the athletes in the study population is depicted in table 24 (Fig. 7). While the average score of all the athletes is 7.21 ± 1.03, the maximum score (7.51 ± 1.18) is observed in district level followed by state level (7.34 ± 1.13) and national level (7.28 ± 0.92) and the minimum score is found in international level. As indicated by the analysis of variances with one way classification (F=5.901, P<0.01), the average score of speed of the athletes in the population varies highly significantly at four different levels. Only three pair combinations of the athletes are found to have their highly significant differences in the average scores of the speed. They are district and international (t=4.093, P<0.01), state and international (t=3.304, P<0.01) and national and

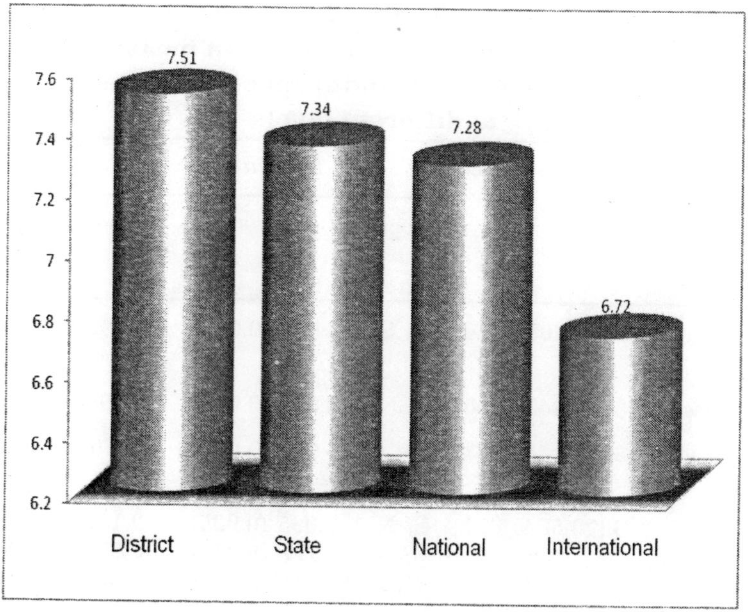

Fig. 7: Variability in Physical Health Measured by Speed of Athletes at Different Levels (In Seconds)

international (t=3.445, P<0.01). The group variances of the four pair combinations say district and international, state and national, state and international and national and international are also found to be highly significant, as evidenced by Levene's statistics, each at 0.01 probability level.

Hence, the above findings can be concluded in the following manner that athletes of district, state and national levels falls under the ranking of fair as their time taken to cover the distance of 50 meter dash lies within the range of 7.6 – 7.0 seconds while the athletes at international level found to be average showing the internal of 6.9 – 6.6 seconds.

Table – 25
Test for variability in physical health measured by cardio respiratory endurance of athletes at different levels

Level (50 cases each)	*Mean* ± *S.D*	*Test-values*		
		Level combination	*t-value*	*Levene's-F*
District (D)	2940.40569.74	D, S	1.938 (0.056)	0.199 (0.656)
State (S)	3150.34512.05	D, N	1.868 (0.065)	0.598 (0.441)
National (N)	3140.74500.33	D, I	4.515**(0.000)	4.770*(0.031)
International (I)	3390.58415.31	S, N	0.095 (0.925)	0.152 (0.698)
		S, I	2.577*(0.011)	4.261*(0.042)
		N, I	2.717**(0.008)	2.509(0.116)
All level	3155.51523.61	ANOVA (F) = 6.720**, P = 0.000		

** indicates significance at* ***0.05*** *level (2-tailed)*
*** indicates significance at* ***0.01*** *level (2-tailed)*
Figures in parentheses indicate P-value.

Table-25 (Fig. 8) also depicts the average scores of the physical health measured by cardio respiratory endurance of the athletes under study at four different levels. The maximum score say 3390.58 ± 415.31 is observed in international level and the minimum one, 2940.40 ± 569.74 is existed in district level. The statistically insignificant difference (t=0.095, P>0.05) scores are found in State level (3150.34 ± 512.05) and national level (3140.74 ± 500.33). However, the athletes of the four levels have, at a glance, a highly significant difference in their scores of the cardio-respiratory endurance (F=6.720, P<0.01). It may be caused by the extreme score value of the international level. The three pair combinations, each involving international level, have statistically significant difference in their scores. They are district and international (t=4.515, P<0.01), state and international (t=2.577, P<0.05) and national and international (t=2.717, P<0.01). In the group variances also, almost the level combinations except two consisting that of international say (D,I) and (N,I) are found to be statistically insignificant difference (P<0.05),manifested in Table 25.

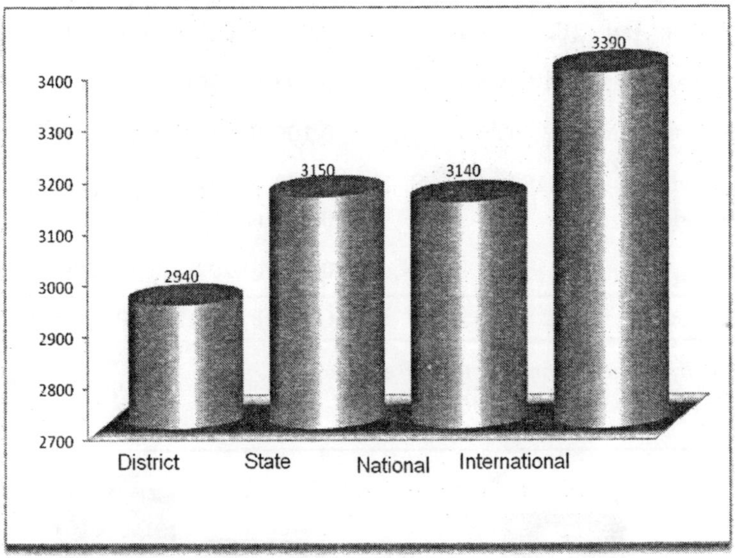

Fig. 8: Variability in Physical Health Measured by Cardio Respiratory Endurance of Athletes at Different Levels (In Meters)

Apart from these statistical findings, their mean scores has been calculated utilizing between minute run and walk calculation of AAHPER Youth Fitness Test. Thus, it can be concluded that all the four levels are included in the same range of moderate.

Table – 26
Test for variability in physical health measured by height of athletes at different levels

Level (50 cases each)	*Mean ± S.D*	*Test-values*		
		Level combination	*t-value*	*Levene's-F*
District (D)	162.925.72	D, S	0.959 (0.340)	4.974* (0.028)
State (S)	161.687.13	D, N	0.293 (0.770)	2.476 (0.143)
National (N)	162.547.15	D, I	0.106 (0.916)	0.519 (0.473)
International (I)	163.1614.96	S, N	0.602 (0.549)	0.290 (0.591)
		S, I	0.631 (0.529)	0.005 (0.942)
		N, I	0.264 (0.792)	0.020(0.889)
All level	162.589.42	ANOVA (F) = 0.235, P = 0.872		

** indicates significance at 0.05 level (2-tailed)*

Figures in parentheses indicate P-value.

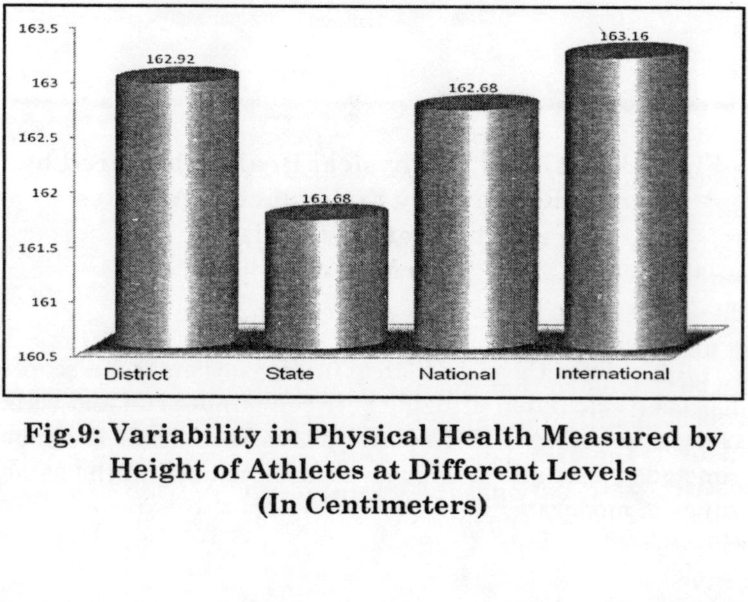

Fig.9: Variability in Physical Health Measured by Height of Athletes at Different Levels (In Centimeters)

Table – 27
Test for variability in physical health measured by weight of athletes at different levels

Level (50 cases each)	*Mean ± S.D*	*Test-values*		
		Level combination	*t-value*	*Levene's-F*
District (D)	51.406.02	D, S	1.347 (0.181)	1.069 (0.304)
State (S)	53.619.93	D, N	1.598 (0.113)	2.349 (0.129)
National (N)	53.647.87	D, I	2.310* (0.023)	0.018 (0.893)
International (I)	54.266.35	S, N	0.016 (0.988)	0.001 (0.973)
		S, I	0.389 (0.698)	0.869 (0.354)
		N, I	0.433 (0.666)	1.842(0.178)
All level	53.237.72	ANOVA (F) = 1.328, P = 0.266		

** indicates significance at 0.05 level (2-tailed)*
Figures in parentheses indicate P-value.

It is worthwhile to observe that the physical health as quantified by both height (F=0.235, P>0.05) and weight (F=1.328, P>0.05) of the athletes in the study population does not vary at four different levels which are depicted in Table 26 (Fig. 9) and Table 27 (Fig. 10) respectively. Utilizing the classical statistics, t-test, all the pair combinations of the athletes at four levels have statistically insignificant differences of heights (P>0.05). In the similar way, the weights of the athletes under study are insignificantly different (P>0.05) at all level pair combinations except one say district and international (t=2.310, P= 0.023). Thus it may be concluded that there is no statistically difference of physical health, measured by height and weight, of the athletes in the study population differentiated by four levels – district, state, national and international.

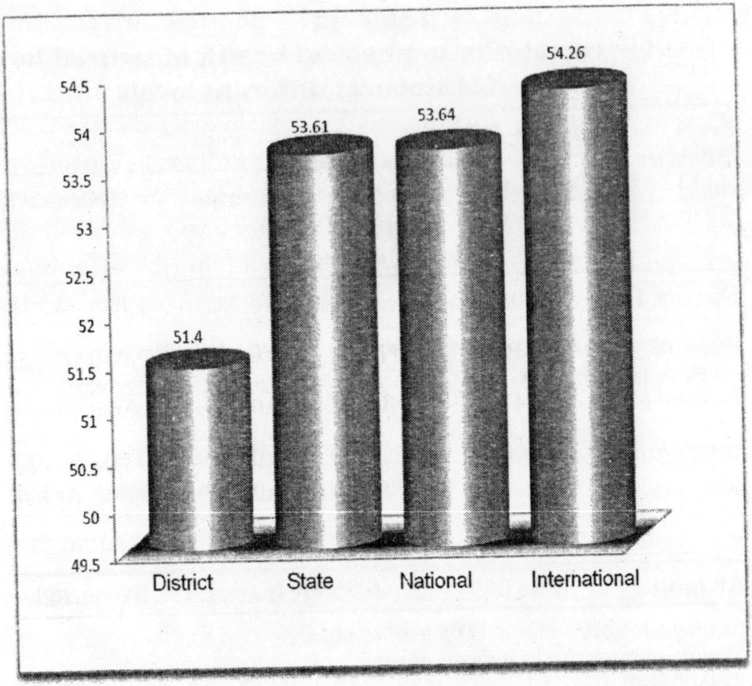

Fig. 10: Variability in Physical Health Measured by Weight of Athletes at Different Levels (In Kilograms)

Besides this statistical finding, with the help of automated Body Mass Index (BMI) calculator, the necessary calculation were also made accordingly by putting all the mean scores of height in centimeter and weight in kilogram. The results of all the different four levels fall within the range of 18.5 to 24.9 which indicates healthy category of BMI key. So, it is again concluded that all the athletes of the study population who are playing at four different levels – district, state, national and international were found to be in the same category of healthy in their height and weight.

Table - 28
Test for variability in physical health measured by muscular strength of athletes with different items

Level (40 cases each)	*Mean ± S.D*	*Test-values*		
		Game combination	*t-value*	*Levene's-F*
Fencing (FC)	13.904.11	FC, SR	0.572 (0.569)	8.184**(0.005)
Soccer (SR)	14.707.93	FC, TK	0.996 (0.322)	12.345**(0.001)
Taekwondo (TK)	15.227.31	FC, ST	1.128 (0.263)	5.417* (0.023)
Sepak Takraw (ST)	12.655.66	FC, JD	2.979**(0.004)	23.261**(0.000)
Judo (JD)	18.569.01	SR, TK	0.302 (0.764)	0.004 (0.950)
		SR, ST	1.334 (0.186)	1.496 (0.225)
		SR, JD	2.033* (0.045)	1.930 (0.169)
		TK, ST	1.757 (0.083)	2.306 (0.133)
		TK, JD	1.822 (0.072)	2.203 (0.142)
		ST, JD	3.515**(0.001)	9.018**(0.004)
All items	15.017.23	ANOVA (F) = 3.970**, P = 0.004		

** indicates significance at 0.05 level (2-tailed)*
*** indicates significance at 0.01 level (2-tailed)*
Figures in parentheses indicate P-value.

The variability in physical health measured by pull-ups for muscular strength of the athletes with different items is again depicted in table 28 (Fig. 11). The muscular strength of athletes is observed at an average of 15.01 with standard deviation (S.D), 7.23. While the highest score value, 18.56$\pm$9.01 found in judo (JD) followed by 15.227.31 in Taekwondo (TK), soccer (SC, 14.70$\pm$7.93) and fencing (FC, 13.90$\pm$4.11) and the lowest value, 12.65$\pm$5.66 is found in Sepak-takraw (ST). This variation is statistically and highly significant at 0.01 probability level as evidenced by ANOVA (F)-value, 3.970 (P=0.004).

In this analysis, only two out of ten item combinations are statistically highly different at 0.01 level of significance as evidenced by t-values, 2.979(FC,JD; P=0.004) and 3.515 (ST,JD; P=0.001) and only one combination, (SR, JD) is found to be significant (t=2.033) at 0.05 significance level, shown in table 28. By computing Levene's F, out of the ten item level combinations, four ones are found to have highly significant difference in their group variances. They are fencing and soccer (8.184, P=0.005), fencing and taekwondo (12.345, P=0.001), fencing and judo (23.261, P=0.000) and sepak-takraw and judo (3.515, P=0.001). Further one item combination, fencing and sepak-takraw is also found different at 0.05 probability level (5.417, P=0.023). Thus it may be concluded that the physical health status, defined by muscular strength, of the athletes in study population varies highly with five different items say fencing, soccer, taekwondo, sepak-takraw and judo.

From the above findings it can now be interpreted that the mean scores of items like fencing and sepak-takraw falls in the interval of 11 – 14 and thus included in the category of good on the other hand, items like taekwondo and judo are in the category of excellent having an interval of 15 and above. But the mean score of soccer lies between the categories of good and excellent exceeding more towards excellent.

Table – 29

Test for variability in physical health measured by strength endurance of athletes with different items

Level (40 cases each)	*Mean ± S.D*	*Test-values*		
		Game combination	*t-value*	*Levene's-F*
Fencing (FC)	44.057.67	FC, SR	1.852 (0.068)	20.453**(0.000)
Soccer (SR)	49.2315.92	FC, TK	7.155**(0.000)	0.022 (0.884)
Taekwondo (TK)	56.507.89	FC, ST	1.044 (0.300)	4.435* (0.038)
Sepak Takraw (ST)	41.5812.88	FC, JD	3.040**(0.003)	0.980 (0.325)
Judo (JD)	49.789.11	SR, TK	2.590*(0.011)	19.294**(0.000)
		SR, ST	2.363* (0.021)	3.722 (0.057)
		SR, JD	0.190 (0.850)	13.303**(0.000)
		TK, ST	6.250**(0.000)	3.976*(0.044)
		TK, JD	3.529**(0.001)	0.709 (0.402)
		ST, JD	3.288**(0.002)	1.784 (0.186)
All items	48.2212.21	ANOVA (F) = 10.711**, P = 0.000		

** indicates significance at 0.05 level (2-tailed)*
*** indicates significance at 0.01 level (2-tailed)*
Figures in parentheses indicate P-value.

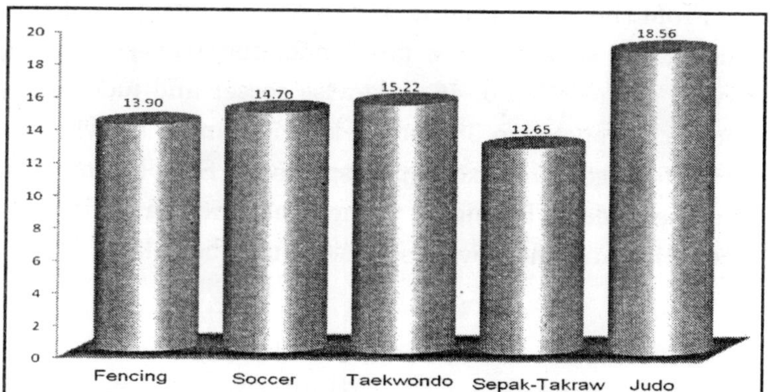

Fig. 11: Variability in Physical Health Measured by Muscular Strength of Athletes with Different Items (Number of Pull-Up)

As measured by bent-knee sit-up test, the strength endurance of the athletes under study varies statistically at five different items (F=10.711, P<0.01) which is manifested in table 29 (Fig. 12). The average score values of the measurement are existed in descending order in taekwondo (56.50 ± 7.89), judo (49.78 ± 9.11), soccer (49.231 ± 5.92), fencing (44.057.67) and sepak-takraw (41.5812.88). Five pair item combinations of the athletes – (FC, TK), (FC, JD), (TK, ST), (TK, JD) AND (ST, JD) are found to be highly significantly different (P<0.01) in their physical health status measured by strength endurance and two such combinations say (SR, TK) and (SR, ST) are also found statistically different (P<0.05). The group variances of the three pair item combinations are existed to be highly and statistically different at 0.01. They are (FC, SR; Levene's F=20.453), (SR, TK; Levene's F=19.294), (SR, JD; Levene's F=13.303). Only two pair item combinations say (FC, ST) and (TK, ST) have also found to have significant difference in their group variances at 0.05 probability level.

From the above finding, it can now be interpreted that fencing and sepak-takraw falls under the average ranking having a repetition of 46. Likewise soccer and judo comes under the repetition 58 and taekwondo under 62 which is meant to be good and excellent respectively. So, it is confirmed that the athletes belonging to the five games have different strength endurance level as measured by bent-knee sit-up.

Table – 30

Test for variability in physical health measured by explosive strength of athletes with different items

Level (40 cases each)	*Mean ± S.D*	*Test-values*		
		Game combination	*t-value*	*Levene's-F*
Fencing (FC)	2.080.33	FC, SR	4.296**(0.000)	13.783**(0.000)
Soccer (SR)	2.350.23	FC, TK	0.002 (0.999)	3.440 (0.067)
Taekwondo (TK)	2.080.41	FC, ST	0.679 (0.499)	2.288 (0.134)
Sepak-Takraw (ST)	2.120.28	FC, JD	1.654 (0.102)	4.282*(0.042)
Judo (JD)	2.190.29	SR, TK	3.662**(0.000)	26.033**(0.000)
		SR, ST	3.995**(0.000)	6.478* (0.013)
		SR, JD	2.732* (0.010)	1.545 (0.218)
		TK, ST	0.591 (0.556)	10.751**(0.002)
		TK, JD	1.442 (0.153)	12.512**(0.001)
		ST, JD	1.081 (0.283)	0.818 (0.368)
All items	2.160.32	ANOVA (F) = 5.315**, P = 0.000		

** indicates significance at 0.05 level (2-tailed)*
*** indicates significance at 0.01 level (2-tailed)*
Figures in parentheses indicate P-value.

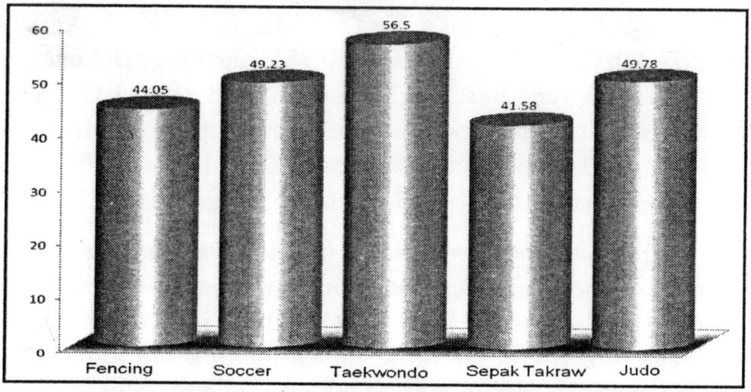

Fig. 12: Variability in Physical Health Measured by Strength Endurance of Athletes with Different Items (Number of Sit Up per Minute)

As an indicator of physical health, the average score of explosive strength measured by standing broad jump of the athletes for all items in the study population is found to be 2.16 ± 0.32. While the maximum score, 2.35 ± 0.23 is observed in soccer followed by judo-2.19 ± 0.29 and sepak-takraw-2.120.28 the minimum score is found in fencing-2.08 ± 0.33 and taekwondo-2.08 ± 0.41. This visible variation is highly and statistically significant at 0.01 probability level as witnessed by F-value, 5.315 (P=0.000), shown in table 30 (Fig. 13).

Out of ten item pair combinations only three ones are noted to be highly significantly different at 0.01 probability level. They are fencing and soccer (t=4.296, P=0.000), soccer and taekwondo (t=3.662, P=0.000) and soccer and sepak-takraw (t=3.995, P=0.000). Only one combination say soccer and judo (t=2.732, P=0.010) is also found statistically different at 0.05 probability level. It may worthwhile be noted that all the item pair combinations having significantly differences consist of the soccer item. It means that the item soccer extremely influences on the variation of explosive strength of the athletes in the analysis. Four item pair combinations viz., (FC,SR; Levene's F=13.783), (SR,TK; Levene's F=26.033), (TK,ST; Levene's F=10.751) and (TK,JD; Levene's F=12.512) have their highly significant (P<0.01) group variances in the study population. Also two item combinations say (FC,JD; Levene's F=4.282) and (SR,ST; Levene's F=6.478) have found statistically different at 5% significance level.

As per the above results, it is also clear that the mean scores of fencing, soccer, taekwondo and sepak-takraw falls under the distance of 2.18 meters which is of a ranking of average. On the other hand judo's mean score alone falls under distance of 2.36 meters which is of a ranking of good. Thus, athletes other than judo have got an average explosive strength and judo itself a good explosive strength as measured by the standing broad jump.

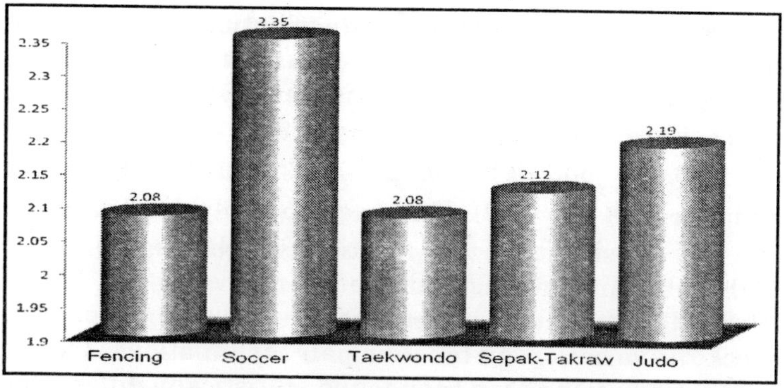

Fig. 13: Variability in Physical Health Measured by Explosive Strength of Athletes with Different Items (In Meters)

Table – 31

Test for variability in physical health measured by agility of athletes with different items

Level (40 cases each)	*Mean ± S.D*	*Test-values*		
		Game combination	*t-value*	*Levene's-F*
Fencing (FC)	9.981.04	FC, SR	6.179**(0.000)	12.830**(0.000)
Soccer (SR)	8.840.53	FC, TK	3.974**(0.000)	6.033**(0.016)
Taekwondo (TK)	9.210.67	FC, ST	4.959**(0.000)	1.402 (0.240)
Sepak Takraw (ST)	8.910.89	FC, JD	4.569**(0.000)	7.984**(0.006)
Judo (JD)	9.110.62	SR, TK	2.706**(0.008)	1.928 (0.169)
		SR, ST	0.401 (0.690)	4.828* (0.031)
		SR, JD	2.081* (0.041)	1.034 (0.312)
		TK, ST	1.698 (0.094)	1.211 (0.274)
		TK, JD	0.676 (0.501)	0.169 (0.682)
		ST, JD	1.178 (0.242)	2.089 (0.152)
All items	9.210.87	ANOVA (F) = 13.948**, P = 0.000		

** indicates significance at 0.05 level (2-tailed)*
*** indicates significance at 0.01 level (2-tailed)*
Figures in parentheses indicate P-value.

Table-31 (Fig. 14) shows the distribution of the average scores of the physical health measured by agility of the athletes at five different items. It is found that the ascending order of average scores as fencing (9.98 ± 1.04), taekwondo (9.21 ± 0.67), judo (9.11 ± 0.62), sepak-takraw (8.91 ± 0.89) and soccer (8.84 ± 0.53). Utilizing the analysis of variance one way classification, the variation is highly significant at 0.01 probability level as evidenced by test value viz., 13.948 (P=0.000). For statistical analysis, t-test is again applied to check the variations in ten item pair combinations. The six pair combinations have been found statistically differences on the physical health status (agility) of the athletes in the analysis. They are fencing and soccer (6.179, P=0.000), fencing and taekwondo (3.974, P=0.000), fencing and sepak-takraw (4.959, P=0.000), fencing and judo (4.569, P=0.000), soccer and taekwondo (2.706, P=0.008) and soccer and judo (2.081, P=0.041) shown in Table 31.

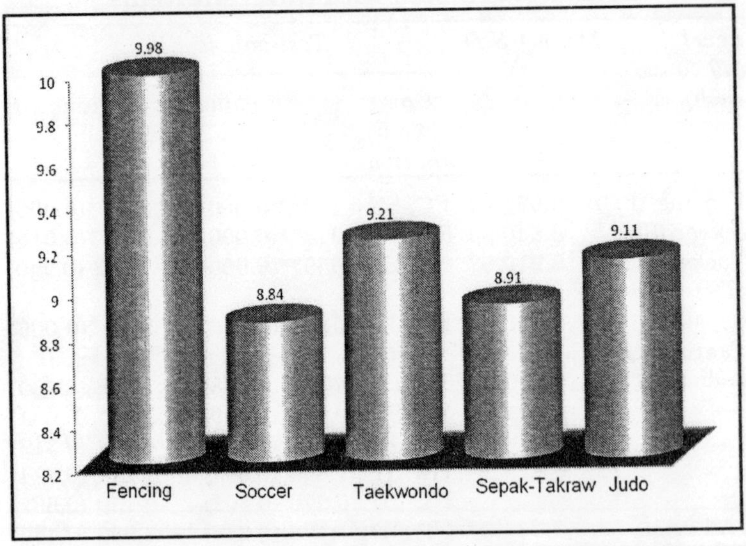

Fig.14: Variability in Physical Health Measured by Agility of Athletes with Different Items (In Seconds)

Taking above findings into consideration, interpretation can be done in the following ways – excellent in the ranking was selected in the athletes of soccer, sepak-takraw and judo having their mean scores of agility falling, at the range of 9.1 – 8.6 seconds. Likewise, athletes of fencing and taekwondo were also marked as average and good in their ranking as their means scores found to be in the internal of 10.3 – 9.8 and 9.17-92 seconds respectively.

Table – 32

Test for variability in physical health measured by speed of athletes with different items

Level (40 cases each)	*Mean ± S.D*	*Test-values*		
		Game combination	*t-value*	*Levene's-F*
Fencing (FC)	7.891.19	FC, SR	5.368**(0.000)	7.746**(0.007)
Soccer (SR)	6.720.68	FC, TK	0.943 (0.349)	0.591 (0.444)
Taekwondo (TK)	7.641.12	FC, ST	5.747**(0.000)	7.365**(0.008)
Sepak-Takraw (ST)	6.650.66	FC, JD	3.184**(0.002)	2.233 (0.139)
Judo (JD)	7.160.81	SR, TK	4.429**(0.000)	23.713**(0.000)
		SR, ST	0.486 (0.628)	0.059 (0.809)
		SR, JD	2.621* (0.011)	3.702 (0.058)
		TK, ST	4.818**(0.000)	24.656**(0.000)
		TK, JD	2.196*(0.031)	10.113**(0.002)
		ST, JD	3.094**(0.003)	3.323 (0.072)
All items	7.211.03	ANOVA (F) = 14.145**, P = 0.000		

** indicates significance at 0.05 level (2-tailed)*
*** indicates significance at 0.01 level (2-tailed)*
Figures in parentheses indicate P-value.

In the study population the distribution of physical health status quantified by speed of the athletes is manifested in table 32 (Fig. 15). While the average score of all the athletes is 7.21 $\pm$ 1.03, the maximum score (7.89 $\pm$ 1.19) is observed in fencing category followed by taekwondo (7.64 $\pm$ 1.12), judo (7.16 $\pm$ 0.81) and soccer (6.72 $\pm$ 0.68), then the minimum score is found in sepak-takraw (6.65 $\pm$ 0.66). As witnessed by F-value, 14.145 (P<0.01), the average score of speed of the athletes in the population varies highly significantly on five different items. Eight item pair combinations of the athletes are found to have their statistically significant differences in the average scores of the speed. They are (FC,SR; t=5.368, P<0.01), (FC,ST; t=5.747, P<0.01), (FC,JD; t=3.184, P<0.01), (SR,TK; t=4.429, P<0.01), (SR,JD; t=2.621, P<0.05), (TK,ST; t=4.818, P<0.01), (TK,JD; t=2.196, P<0.05) and (ST,JD; t=3.094, P<0.01).

To investigate the significant variations on group variances of the athletes on item combinations, Levene's F is again computed. It is found that the five item combinations are found to be highly significant each at 1% significance level of probability. The pair combinations are (FC,SR; 5.368, P=0.007), (FC,ST; 7.365, P=0.008), (SR,TK; 23.713, P<0.000), (TK,ST; 24.656, P=0.000) and (TK,JD; 10.113, P=0.002), shown in Table 32.

In continuation to the above findings, it is interpreted that the athletes belonging to fencing and taekwondo have a ranking of poor in their speed as the athletes of these two games cover 50 meter dash in the internal of 10.6 – 7.7 seconds. Likewise, soccer and sepak-takraw falls under average having a mean score between 6.9 – 6.6 seconds. Lastly, the athletes belonging to judo are found to be fair in their ranking with their mean scores within the range of 7.56 – 7.0 seconds.

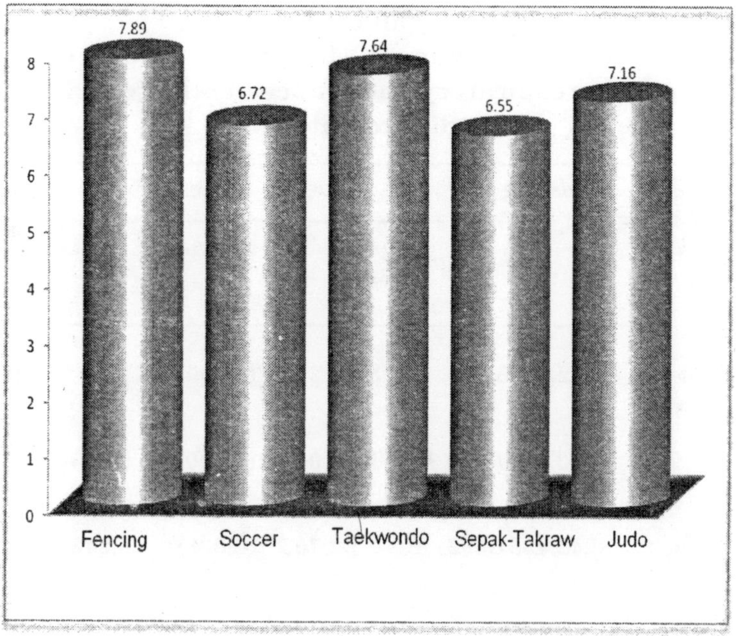

Fig. 15: Variability in Physical Health Measured by Speed of Athletes with Different Items (In Seconds)

Table-33 (Fig. 16) highlights the average scores of the physical health measured by cardio respiratory endurance of the athletes under study in five different items – fencing (FC), soccer (SR), taekwondo (TK), sepak-takraw (ST) and judo (JD). In this analysis the average score of the physical health (cardio respiratory endurance) varies differently (F=15.912, P=0.000) with the five different items which is highly significant at 0.01 probability level. The maximum score say 3590.73 $\pm$ 279.09 is observed in the item soccer followed by its taekwondo (3242.43 $\pm$ 510.99) and the minimum score, 2802.95 $\pm$ 457.50 is existed on fencing category while the average score value is 3155.51 $\pm$ 523.61.

Table – 33
Test for variability in physical health measured by cardio-respiratory endurance of athletes with different items

Level (40 cases each)	*Mean ± S.D*	*Test-values*		
		Game combination	*t-value*	*Levene's-F*
Fencing (FC)	2802.95457.50	FC, SR	9.297**(0.000)	14.883**(0.000)
Soccer (SR)	3590.73279.09	FC, TK	4.052**(0.000)	1.835 (0.179)
Taek-wondo (TK)	3242.43510.99	FC, ST	2.706**(0.008)	0.242 (0.624)
Sepak-Takraw (ST)	3073.70437.12	FC, JD	2.312*(0.023)	0.373 (0.543)
Judo (JD)	3067.78561.54	SR, TK	3.783**(0.000)	30.534**(0.000)
		SR, ST	6.305**(0.000)	10.767**(0.002)
		SR, JD	5.274**(0.000)	12.892**(0.001)
		TK, ST	1.587 (0.117)	3.433 (0.068)
		TK, JD	1.455 (0.150)	0.183 (0.670)
		ST, JD	0.053 (0.958)	0.995 (0.322)
All items	3155.51523.61	ANOVA (F) = 15.912**, P = 0.000		

** indicates significance at 0.05 level (2-tailed)*
*** indicates significance at 0.01 level (2-tailed)*
Figures in parentheses indicate P-value.

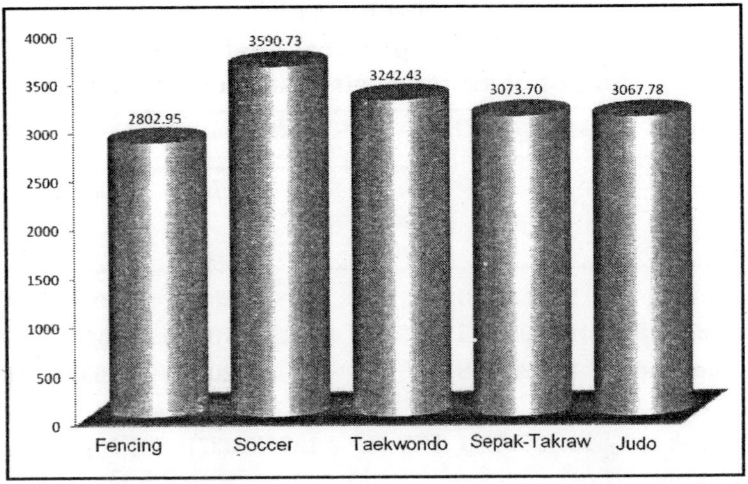

Fig. 16: Variability in Physical Health Measured by Cardio Respiratory Endurance of Athletes with Different Items (In Meters)

The statistically significant difference of physical health status of the athletes defined by cardio respiratory endurance exists on seven item pair combinations. They are (FC,SR; t=9.297, P<0.01), (FC,TK; t=4.052, P<0.01), (FC,ST; t=2.706, P<0.01), (FC,JD; t=2.312, P<0.05), (SR,TK; t=3.783, P<0.01), (SR,ST; t=6.305, P<0.01) and (SR,JD; t=5.274, P<0.01). The four pair combinations among the ten namely fencing and soccer, soccer and taekwondo, soccer and sepak-takraw and soccer and judo have statistically difference in their group variances, highly significant at 1% significance level of probability by utilizing Levene's statistics depicted in Table 33.

In addition to this statistical analysis, the mean scores of the five different games were also calculated by twelve minute run and walk calculation for cardio respiratory test of AAHPER Youth Fitness Test. Further it was detected that games like fencing, taekwondo, sepak-takraw and judo are found to be in the moderate range while soccer under the high range.

Table - 34
Test for variability in physical health measured by height of athletes with different items

Level (40 cases each)	*Mean ± S.D*	*Test-values*		
		Game combination	*t-value*	*Levene's-F*
Fencing (FC)	163.685.10	FC, SR	1.148 (0.254)	0.591 (0.444)
Soccer (SR)	164.934.63	FC, TK	0.262 (0.794)	11.196**(0.001)
Taekwondo (TK)	163.288.18	FC, ST	1.281 (0.204)	2.765 (0.100)
Sepak-Takraw (ST)	160.1516.64	FC, JD	2.127*(0.037)	1.907 (0.171)
Judo (JD)	160.856.67	SR, TK	1.111 (0.270)	16.058**(0.000)
		SR, ST	1.748 (0.084)	3.561 (0.063)
		SR, JD	3.174**(0.002)	4.163*(0.045)
		TK, ST	1.066 (0.290)	0.207 (0.651)
		TK, JD	1.453 (0.150)	3.1440 (0.080)
		ST, JD	0.247 (0.806)	1.349 (0.249)
All items	162.589.42	ANOVA (F) = 1.844, P = 0.122		

** indicates significance at 0.05 level (2-tailed)*
*** indicates significance at 0.01 level (2-tailed)*
Figures in parentheses indicate P-value

It is worthwhile to observe that the physical health as quantified by both height (F=1.844, P>0.05) and weight (F=2.259, P>0.05) of the athletes in the study population does not vary with five different items which are depicted in table 34 (Fig. 17) and table 35 respectively. While the average weight of the athletes under study is 162.58 ± 9.42 cm, some visible variations on the height of the athletes are found to be 164.93 ± 4.63 cm in soccer, 163.68 ± 5.10 cm in fencing, 163.28 ± 8.18 cm in taekwondo, 160.85 ± 6.67 cm in judo and the minimum-160.15 ± 6.64 cm in sepak- takraw. The visible difference in the weight of the athletes are also seen with different items while its average value is 53.23 ± 7.72 kg., shown in table 35 (Fig. 18).

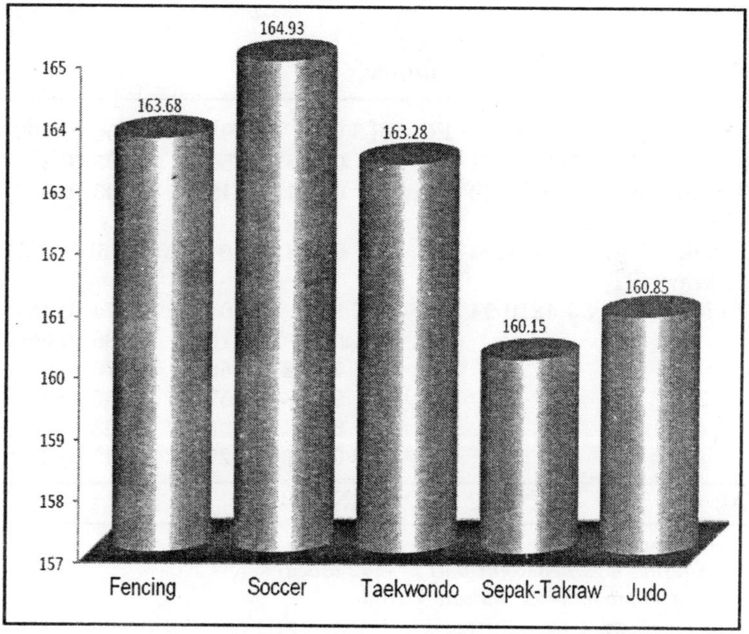

Fig. 17: Variability in Physical Health Measured by Height of Athletes with Different Items (In Centimeters)

Like the findings given by classical statistics, it is also observed that height of the athletes of the five different games of the study say fencing, soccer, taekwondo, sepak-takraw and judo were found to be in the same category – healthy as evidenced by Body Mass Index (BMI) calculator. Calculation has been worked out with their mean scores resulting within the range of 18.5 – 24.9 which indicates the healthy category of the BMI key. So, it is obvious that height of the athletes of the above games does not differ.

Table – 35
Test for variability in physical health measured by weight of athletes with different items

Level (40 cases each)	*Mean ± S.D*	*Test-values*		
		Game combination	*t-value*	*Levene's-F*
Fencing (FC)	52.255.82	FC, SR	3.051**(0.003)	0.150 (0.700)
Soccer (SR)	56.235.83	FC, TK	0.455 (0.650)	2.496 (0.118)
Taekwondo (TK)	51.538.22	FC, ST	0.361 (0.719)	0.003 (0.957)
Sepak-Takraw (ST)	52.735.94	FC, JD	0.594 (0.554)	4.075*(0.047)
Judo (JD)	53.4210.94	SR, TK	2.949**(0.004)	1.774 (0.187)
		SR, ST	2.659*(0.010)	0.186 (0.668)
		SR, JD	1.433 (0.156)	3.370 (0.070)
		TK, ST	0.748 (0.457)	2.532 (0.116)
		TK, JD	0.873 (0.385)	0.603 (0.440)
		ST, JD	0.351 (0.727)	4.114* (0.046)
All items	53.237.72	ANOVA (F) = 2.259, P = 0.064		

** indicates significance at 0.05 level (2-tailed)*
*** indicates significance at 0.01 level (2-tailed)*
Figures in parentheses indicate P-value.

Utilizing the classical statistics, t-test, all the item pair combinations of the athletes except two have statistically insignificant differences of heights (P>0.05). The two significant values are found in fencing and judo (t=2.127, P<0.05) and soccer and judo (t=3.174, P<0.01) which is depicted in table 34. In the similar way, the weights of the athletes under study are insignificantly different (P>0.05) at all item pair combinations except three ones. The three pair combinations are fencing and soccer (t=3.051, P<0.01), soccer and taekwondo (t=2.949, P<0.01) and soccer and sepak-takraw (t=2.659, P<0.05), shown in table 35 (Fig. 18). Thus it may be concluded that there is no statistically difference of physical health, measured by height and weight, of the athletes in the study population differentiated by five different items – say fencing, soccer, taekwondo, sepak-takraw and judo.

Apart from the statistical point of view, with reference to that of Body Mass Index (BMI) calculator, the necessary calculation has been made by putting their mean scores of height in centimeter and weight in kilogram and their results comes under the range of 18.5 to 24.9 showing healthy category of BMI key. So, it can also be finalized that all the athletes belonging to five different games of the present study falls under the category of healthy.

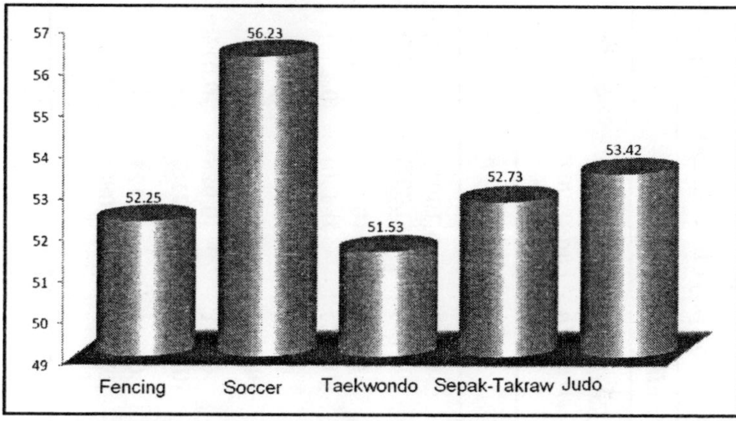

Fig.18: Variability in Physical Health Measured by Weight of Athletes with Different Items (In Kilograms)

In Table-36, the relationship between physical health and psychological health indicators of the athletes are investigated with zero order correlation and their P-values of the test statistics (t-test). The physical health status is quantified by eight indicators – agility, muscular strength, explosive strength, strength endurance, speed, cardio respiratory endurance, height and weight. And psychological health is also defined by eight indicators viz., anxiety, stress,

Table – 36

Zero order correlation matrix of psychological and physical health indicators

Psychological health indicator	*Physical health indicator*				*Physical health indicator*			
	Agility	*Muscular strength*	*Explosive strength*	*Strength endurance*	*Speed*	*Cardio respiratory endurance*	*Height*	*Weight*
1	*2*	*3*	*4*	*5*	*6*	*7*	*8*	*9*
Anxiety	-0.063 (0.378)	0.187** (0.008)	-0.022 (0.754)	0.190** (0.007)	-0.053 (0.457)	0.010 (0.885)	-0.078 (0.272)	0.075 (0.290)
Stress	0.099 (0.164)	0.023 (0.745)	-0.088 (0.217)	0.055 (0.439)	0.081 (0.253)	-0.078 (0.273)	-0.081 (0.254)	-0.030 (0.671)
Depression	-0.117 (0.100)	0.071 (0.317)	-0.032 (0.650)	0.162* (0.022)	-0.112 (0.115)	0.015 (0.837)	-0.030 (0.674)	-0.032 (0.652)
Regression	0.047 (0.508)	-0.089 (0.212)	-0.131 (0.645)	-0.026 (0.718)	-0.015 (0.836)	-0.044 (0.540)	-0.030 (0.669)	-0.027 (0.700)
Guilt	-0.063 (0.377)	-0.001 (0.989)	0.030 (0.674)	0.121 (0.088)	-0.019 (0.786)	0.039 (0.588)	-0.068 (0.337)	0.024 (0.738)

(Contd...)

1	2	3	4	5	6	7	8	9
Fatigue	0.122 (0.086)	0.088 (0.215)	-0.203** (0.004)	0.039 (0.582)	0.050 (0.479)	-0.192** (0.007)	-0.058 (0.415)	-0.008 (0.911)
Extraversion	0.054 (0.450)	-0.063 (0.379)	-0.100 (0.161)	-0.117 (0.100)	0.061 (0.390)	-0.162* (0.022)	-0.159* (0.025)	-0.079 (0.267)
Arousal	0.031 (0.667)	-0.058 (0.412)	-0.069 (0.331)	0.090 (0.207)	-0.015 (0.837)	-0.021 (0.771)	-0.062 (0.385)	-0.025 (0.728)

Correlation is significant at the **0.05 level (2-tailed)*

***Correlation is significant at the **0.01** level (2-tailed)*

Figures in parentheses indicate P-value.

depression, regression, guilt, fatigue, extraversion and arousal.

It is observed that agility has no any linear relationship with all the indicators of psychological health as indicated by r-values (P>0.05). In this analysis, muscular strength, as a measure of physical health is positively and linearly related with anxiety (r=0.187, P=0.008), which is highly significant at 0.01 probability level. Explosive strength is also found to be negatively related with fatigue, as indicated by highly significant zero order correlation, -0.203 (P=0.004). Besides, strength endurance of the athletes varies positively and linearly with two psychological health indicators say anxiety (r=0.190, P<0.01) and depression (r=0.162, P<0.05). No significant linear correlations between speed (physical health) and psychological indicators are detected in the study population. However, cardio respiratory endurance is found to vary negatively and significantly with fatigue (r= -0.192, P<0.01) and extraversion (r= -0.162, P<0.05). The height of the athletes also varies with extraversion negatively and linearly as its r-value (-0.159). It is significant at 5% level of significance. There is no significant correlation between weight and psychological health indicators in the study population.

Thus, from the above findings the hypothesis of the study can also be tested whether there is no significant relationship between psychological health and physical health of the athletes of Manipur. So, physical indicators like agility, speed and weight are found to have no significant relationship with that of any of the psychological variables leading to the acceptance of the hypothesis. On the other hand, significant relationship has been found between muscular strength and anxiety, strength endurance with anxiety and depression, explosive strength and fatigue, cardio-respiratory endurance with both fatigue and extraversion and finally height with that of extraversion. Thus, according to this relationship the above hypothesis is rejected. But other than the relationship amongst the above mentioned indicators of both physical and psychological health, the remaining indicators are found to have no significant relationship. So, in this regard it clearly supports the hypothesis of the study.

5

Summary, Conclusion and Recommendations

The main purpose of the study was to compare and find out the relationship between psycho-physical health of the athletes of Manipur at various levels in respect of five games confirming to sample size. The subjects were altogether 200 ranging from an age group of seventeen to twenty three years. They were selected from various games viz. fencing, soccer, taekwondo, sepak-takraw and judo who participated in the district, state, national and international levels from the different parts of Manipur.

The sample was selected through purposive method of sampling. It was divided into four different groups comprising of 50 athletes each in the district, state, national and international levels. From each level 10 subjects were selected representing altogether 40 subjects from one particular game.

The variables taken into consideration included psychological variables namely anxiety, stress, depression, regression, fatigue, guilt, extraversion, arousal and physical fitness components namely height, weight, agility, cardio-respiratory endurance, explosive strength, muscular endurance, speed and strength endurance. The reliability of data was ensured by establishing the instrument reliability, reliability of tests and subjects' reliability.

The selection of test was based on the expert's opinion, administrative feasibility, time factor nature of the subjects and facilities available to conduct the test. For the measurement of psychological health the Eight State Questionnaire [8SQ] originally prepared by Barton, Cattell and Curran was used. The physical fitness levels of the athletes were measured with the help of AAHPER Youth Fitness Test. The six different physical fitness components of the athletes namely muscular strength, strength endurance, explosive strength, agility, speed and cardio-respiratory endurance were measured by the test items viz. pull-up, bent knee sit ups, standing broad jump, shuttle run, 50 meter dash and 12 minute run or walk respectively. In addition to this, physical health characterized by height and weight of athletes were also measured through standardized equipments namely Stedeometre and electronic weighing machine respectively on the context of the study.

For administering the tests for the present study, the officials of different sports associations, youth affairs and sports department and sports authority of India N.E. region were contacted and requested to allow their athletes to serve as the subjects of this study also including the individual athletes. According to their availability of time, the athletes were made respond at the practice area of the respective games during their practice sessions. The necessary guidelines and instructions of the tests to be followed in the study were given to the athletes. They were also given assurance that their responses would be kept confidential and would not be used for any other purpose. Thus, the required data for psychological health were collected through the means of questionnaires. Moreover for the physical health the test items mentioned in the AAHPER Youth Fitness Test including height and weight were administered with the assistance of respective coaches.

The analysis of data for the present study has been furnished through the SPSS (statistical package for social sciences, version 11.5). The classical statistics viz., r, t, ANOVA-F, Levene's F were utilized on the average score values of indicators of interest of the study population. By applying t-test, the pair combinations with two levels and games at a time, the components of indicators irrespective of psychological health and physical health of the athletes were also analysed with their significant differences. It was examined at 0.05 and 0.01 levels of probability. Besides, the variations in the indicators at four levels according to the five different games were also advocated by utilizing the ANOVA-F. The variations in group variances of the athletes differentiated by four different levels as well as the five different games have also been assessed with the help of Levene's F-statistics. The interrelationship among the indicators of physical health and psychological health were determined with product moment correlations (r) and differences were measured by t-test thereon.

The various psychological variables regarding the level-wise consideration the psychological health as measured by anxiety were found to be in slightly deviant for national and international levels. But that of district and state levels fall in between average and slightly deviant. Thus, significant difference has been detected among the levels. Likewise, the athletes' psychological health as measured by stress, depression, regression, fatigue and extraversion were all found to be under average for all the various levels. Thus, no significant difference has been noted among them. Meanwhile, for guilt and arousal all the levels were found to be in slightly deviant.

Regarding game-wise variation, as per the measurement carried by stress, regression, fatigue and extraversion all the games were found to be in the same category that is average leading to have no significant difference. In contrary to this psychological health measured by anxiety depression, guilt and arousal were all included under slightly deviant for all the various games.

The physical health as measured by the various physical components has got significant difference among the athletes from different levels belonging to various games. Muscular strength differs from district level which was good while that of state, national and international levels which were found to be excellent. Out for the five games, fencing and sepak-takraw falls under good whereas soccer, taekwondo and judo fall under excellent. For strength endurance, district level comes under average, state and national levels under good and finally international level under excellent. Moreover, for game-wise variation, fencing and sepak-takraw were included in average, soccer and judo in good and taekwondo alone in excellent. Again, the explosive strength was found to be in average for all the levels except for international level which is good. Likewise, fencing, soccer, taekwondo and sepak-takraw falls under average except for judo which is good. In the case of agility, district and state levels were in good while that of national and international levels were in average. But for the games, fencing comes within average, taekwondo under good while soccer, sepak-takraw and judo under excellent. In the condition for speed, except for international level which was in average all the other remaining levels were in fair. But for games, fencing and taekwondo were found to be in poor, judo in fair and finally soccer and sepak-takraw in average. Again, in regard to cardio-respiratory endurance all the athletes from four levels were altogether found in the range of moderate. As for the games, fencing, taekwondo, sepak-takraw and judo were all included in moderate but soccer in high range. Lastly, the athletes were all found to be in healthy condition as measured by height and weight.

Again, for the comparison between physical components and the psychological components significant relationship has been found such as anxiety vs. muscular strength (0.187), anxiety vs. strength endurance (0.190), depression vs. strength endurances (0.162) and fatigue vs. explosive strength (-0.203). But for the other remaining comparisons, no significant relationship was found.

Conclusion

Based on the above findings of the study, the following conclusions could be drawn:

1. No significant difference has been detected among the athletes of the four levels as measured by stress, depression, regression, fatigue and extraversion.
2. Significant difference has been found among the athletes of four levels as measured by anxiety.
3. No significant difference has also been detected among the athletes of all the levels as measured by guilt and arousal.
4. No significant difference has been observed among the athletes of five different games as indicated by all the eight psychological indicators.
5. The athletes' physical health as measured by height and weight has no significant difference considering level-wise and game-wise.
6. Cardio-respiratory endurance gave no difference among the athletes at various levels.
7. Except the above mentioned physical components according to these levels or game-wise consideration, all the remaining physical indicators gave no significant difference to the athletes of the present study.

8. Significant relationship has been found between anxiety and muscular strength, anxiety and strength endurance, regression and strength endurance and lastly fatigue and explosive strength.

Recommendations

In accordance to the results found in this study, the following recommendations can be made:

1. Performance of athletes depend to a great extent upon the psychological variables. As a result, a stable state of mind is very important. Thus, proper training should be given to the athletes to cope up with any sorts of psychological problems.
2. Athletes need to be physically strong and active. So, more practice, training and even proper equipments must be provided according to their concerned games.
3. The findings also showed significant relationship between physical health and psychological health. So, special training must be given to them to strongly face any mental worries thus increasing their self-confidence and self-esteem.
4. Similar study could be conducted on psychological and physical indicators other than those employed in this study.
5. Similar study could be undertaken on the sportspersons belonging to different games other than fencing, taekwondo, sepak-takraw, soccer and judo.
6. Study could also be employed on other sportspersons from another state of India.

Bibliography

Books

AAHPER,: *Planning Facilities for Athletics, Physical Education and Recreation,* Washington, D.C: AAHPER Publication, 1979.

American Association for Health, Physical Education and Recreation, *Aahper Youth Fitness Test Manual*, Virginia, D.C.: AAPHER Publication, 1976.

Bach Haver Ervin, *The Propagation of Dynamics in School,* Athens: Hellanic Olympic Committee, 1967, p.2.

Barrow Harold M. and Ganic P. Brown, "Man and Movement" *Principles of Physical Education,* Fourth Edition, Philadelphia: Lea and Febiger Co., 1983, p.167.

Bell, Keith, F. "Championship Thinking" *Athletes Guide to Winning Performance in all Sports,* London: Prentice hall Inc., 1982, p.152.

Bucher Charles A. and West Debora: *Foundation of Physical Education and Sports,* St. Louis: The C.V. Mosby Company, Tenth Edition, 1987, Pp.56-57.

Butt, Dorcas Susan, *Psychology of Sports,* U.S.A.: Van Nostrand Reinhold Company Inc., 1987.

Clark, H. Harrison, *Application of Measurement to Health and Physical Education,* Englewood Cliffs, N.J: Prentice Hall, Inc., 1976, Pp.173, 203.

Cox. Richard H. *Sports Psychology, Concept and Application,* Dedugue Lowa William C. Brown Publisher, 1985.

Cratty, Brayant J., "Anxiety and Performance", *Movement Behaviour and Motor Learning,* Philadelphia: Lea and Febiger, 1975.

Curran, Cattell and Barton, *Manual of Eight State questionnaire [8SQ],* 1976, Published and reprinted in India by the Psycho Centre, New Delhi, 1989.

Donald A. Chu, *Explosive Power Strength, Complex Training for Maximum Results,* Human Kinetics Publishers Inc., 1994.

Dr. Micheal Moredith, *The Relaxation and Stress Reduction Workbook,* Fifth Edition, 2001.

F.G. Guigan Mc., *Experimental Psychology, Methodology of Research,* Prentice Hall of India, New Delhi, 1990.

Fleishman, Edwin A., *The Structure and Measurement of Physical Fitness,* Englewood Cliffs, Philadelphia: W.B.Saunders Company, 1975, p.144.

Frost, Reuben, B., *Psychological Concept Applied to Physical Education and Coaching,* Mass Achuestts: Addition Wesley, 1971.

F.J. Guigan Mc., *Experimental Psychology, Methodology of Research,* Prentice Hall of India, New Delhi, 1990.

Gupta Santosh, *Research Methodology, A Statistical Technique,* Deep and Deep Publication F-159, New Delhi, 2001.

Hockey, Robert V., Physical Fitness *The Pathway for Healthful Living,* St. Louis: The C.V. Mosby Company, 1973, Pp.93-94.

Jack, H. Liewellyn and Judy A. Blucker, *"Anxiety and Performance", Psychology of Coaching: Theory and Application,* Delhi: Surjeet Publication, 1982, p.1.

John, M. Silva III and Robert L. Weinberg, *Psychological Foundation of Sports;* University of Carolina; 1984.

Johnson, Barry L. and Nelson, Jack K., *Practical Measurement for Evaluation in Physical Education;* Third Edition, Bergis Publishing Company, 1969, p.215.

Kamlesh, M.L., *Methodology of Research in Physical Education and Sports,* Metropolitan Book Co. Pvt. Ltd., 1994.

Kamlesh, M.L., *Psychology of Physical Education and Sports,* New Delhi: Multropllitan Books Company Pvt. Ltd., 1983, p.17.

Mangal S.K., *Educational Psychology,* Illinois: Human Kinetics Publishers, 1982.

Mathews, Donald K., *Measurement in Physical Education,* Philadelphia: W.B. Saunders Company, 1978, Pp.4-5, 144.

Mc. Gee and Barrow, *A Practical Approach to Measurement in Physical Education,* Philadelphia: Lea and Febiger; 1964, p.113.

Mc. Cloy C.M. and Norman D. Young, *Test and Measurement in Health and Physical Education,* New York, 1954.

Methrens, William A. and Lehmann, Iruia J., *Measurement and Evaluation in Education and Psychology,* 2nd Edition, New York: Holt, Riwheart and Winston, 1978.

Shadu, A.N. and Amarjit Singh, *Research Methodology in Social Sciences,* Himalayan Publishing House, Bombay, 1996.

Sharma R.A., *Foundation of Physical Education and Research,* Loyal Book Department, Meerut, 1996.

Sharma V.D.: *Introduction to Physical and Health Education,* Avichal Publishing Company, New Delhi 2000, Pp.1-4.

Silva, John M. and Weinberg, Robert S., *Psychological Foundation of Sport,* Champaign Human Kinetic Publishes Inc., 1984.

Singer, N. Robert: *Myths and Truths in Sports Psychology,* New York: Harper and Row Publisher, 1975, p.4.

Singh Agyajit: *Sports Psychology: A Study of Indian Sportsmen,* Delhi: Friends Publication, 1992, Pp.36, 37.

Uppal, A.K., *Physical Fitness: How to Develop,* New Delhi: Friends Publications, 1996, p.6.

Willgoose, Carle, *Evaluation in Health Education and Physical Education,* New York: McGraw Hill Book Co., Inc., 1961, p.16.

Journal and Periodicals

Adedoja, T.A.: "The Relationship between Anxiety and Level of Aspiration among College Physical Education Male Students", *Completed Research in Health, Physical Education and Recreation,* 24(1982):25.

Alan J. Pearce et al.: "Characteristics of selected and non-selected elite junior Australian footballers", *Journal of Sports Science and Medicine* (2007), Suppl. 10:p. 188.

Amusa Latteef: "The Relationship between Soccer Playing Ability and Selected Measures of Structures on Physical Psychological Performance in College Men", *Completed Research in Health Physical Education and Recreation,* 21(1989):201.

B. Kareng and Nicholas L. Collete Hoglund: "Shame, Guilt and Anger in College, Students Expose to Abusive Family Environment", *Journal of Family Violence,* 10:2(June 1995):141-157.

Bawa, G.S. and Nakarmi M.L.: "A Comparative Study of Physical Activities Levels of Nepalese Gymnastic Girls and Nepalese School Girls Ranging from 10 to 13 Years" *Journal of Sports and Sports Sciences,* 26(1):13(2003).

Borysiuk Z.: "Complex Evaluation of Fencers Predisposition in Three Stages of Sport development", *Biology of Sport,* 23:4-53,2006.

Dalerose M Neaman: Anxiety Reduction and Performance Enhancement for Female Competitive Gymnasts", *Dissertation Abstracts International,* 154:7(Jan. 1994):2516-A.

Debray, Parthasrathi and Dey S.K., "A Comparative Study of Maximal Aerobic Power of School Boys of East and North-East Regions of India", *Indian Periodicals,* 3:40(2003):105-114.

Edward Charles and Aldrich: "An Investigation into the Relationship between Operative Study Strategies Self-efficacy, Non-curricular Activities Erickson's Hierarchy of Physiological Development and Two Level of Academic Achievement in Junior High School Students", *Dissertation Abstract International,* 59:6 (Dec. 1998):1884-A.

Haley Ray Philip:"A Comparative Analysis of Selected Motor Fitness Test Performance of Elementary School Boys", *Dissertation Abstracts International,* 46:2 (Aug. 1985):373.

Jones G. and Swain A.:"Relationship between Sports Achievement Orientation and Competition State Anxiety", *Sports Psychology,* (U.S.A.) 6:1(March 1992):42-54.

Karkare Ajay and Agashe C.O., "Comparative Study between Tribal and Non-Tribal Sports Persons of Chattisgarh Related to their Motor Fitness", *Tribal Health Bulletin,* vol.9(May 2004), nos. 1 & 2.

Leweiz: "An Approach on a Development of Sports Psychology in China", Sports Sciences: *Journal of China Sports Science Society,*(CHN)12:4(1992):83-86 cited in Sports Documentation Monthly Bulletin 22(July, August 1992):40.

Leszek Cicirko et al.: "General and special physical fitness levels in young football players", *Journal of Sports Science and Medicine",* (2007) Suppl. 10:p. 187.

Moh, Leakhena and Nou: "Stress Social Support, Coping and Psychological Adjustment of Khmer University, College and Technical Students in Modern Day Cambodia", *Dissertation Abstracts International,* 63:6 (Dec. 2002):2383-A.

PK. Dasgupta, Mukhopadhyay and De AK., "A Study of Cardio-Pulmonary Efficiency in Different Categories of Runners", *Indian Journal of Physiology and Pharmacology,* 44:2(April 2002): 220-4.

R. Kristen and Boughman: The Social-Psychological Benefits of Sports and Fitness Identities, *Dissertation Abstracts International,* 61:7(September 2002):1180-A.

Robins Callaway William: "Albana Motor Fitness and Health Related Fitness Norms: Ages 6 – 14", *Dissertation Abstracts International,* 46:1(July 1985):101.

Seiler R.: "Performance Enhancement: Psychological Approach", *Soviet Sports Review,* (U.S.A.)1:2 (1992): 29-45C, Cited in Sports Documentation Monthly Bulletin 22:9(September 1992):41.

Singh H., Singh J. and Singh S.: "Comparison of Physical Fitness Between Senior and Junior Group of Hockey Girls", *Journal of Sports and Sports Sciences,* 26(1):45, (2003).

Smith and J. Randy: "The Relationship of Anger and Anxiety to Depression: Multidimentional Perspective",

Dissertation Abstracts International, 54:3 (September 1993):822-A.

Sook Jung and Kim: "Effect of Taekwondo Exercise on the Psychological well Being of School Children and Young Adults", *Dissertation Abstracts International,* 64:2 (August 2003):441-A.

W. Donald Campbell: The Relationship of Selected Measures of Physical Performance and Structure of Quality of Performance in Collegiate Football", *Completed Research in Health, Physical Education and Recreation,* 21(1980):143.

W.F.Beiter: "Prediction of Football Playing Ability", *Completed Research in Health Physical Education and Dance,* 23(1981):181.

Unpublished Theses

A.V. Thomas: "Construction of a Specific Test Battery of Motor Fitness for Hockey Players", *Unpublished M.Phil. Dissertation,* Jiwaji University, 1992.

Debnath, Monika: "Psychological Profiles of National Women Gymnasts, *Unpublished Master's Thesis,* Jiwaji University, 1989.

Dey Nath Atendra: "Study of Anthropometric Measurement and Body Composition of High and Low Cardio-Respiratory Fitness of Boys", *Unpublished Ph.D. Thesis,* Jiwaji University, 1986.

Gojendra Prakash: "Comparison fo Selected Physiological and Physical Fitness of Soccer and Cricket Players", *Unpublished Master's Thesis,* L.N.C.P.E., Gwalior, Jiwaji University, 1984.

K. Kumaran Prasana: "Psychological Factors Influencing the Participation of Females in Physical Activity", *Unpublished Ph.D. Thesis,* Jiwaji University, 2001.

Modak Pintu, "Comparative Effect of Induced Mental and Physical Fatigue of Different Duration on the Performance of Psycho-Motor Task Among Gymnasts at Different Age Level", *Unpublished Ph.D. Thesis,* Jiwaji University, 1994.

Nandi Santimoy: "Anxiety: Its Effects upon Performance on Soccer Skill Test Requiring Gross Motor Skills", *Unpublished Master's Thesis,* Jiwaji University, 1989.

Vaz Wilfred Leons: "Investigation of Selected Anthropmetric Characteristics and Physical Fitness Components as Predictions of Performance in Judo", *Unpublished Ph.D. Thesis,* Jiwaji University, 1993.

Miscellaneous

Alan D. Dobbins, "Cricket", *Encyclopedia of Sports Sciences and Medicines,* 4th Edition.

Clarence L. Barnhart and Robert K. Barnhart, "Definition of Athletes", *The World Book Dictionary,* 2000.

Edgerton, Jane E., *American Psychiatric Glossary,* 7th Edition, Washington D.C.; American Psychiatric Press, 1994.

The American Heritage, *Dictionary of English Language,* 4th Edition, Published by Houghton Miffler Company, 2000.

www.mindtools.com/stress/stressdefinition.htm.

www.abcbook.com/abnormalpsychology.html.

www.sportsfilter.com.

www.exrx.net.html.

www.<web.concernutrition.info.com>.

www.amazone.com.

APPENDIX - A

THE PSYCHO CENTER
8 STATE QUESTIONNAIRES
[8SQ]
FORM A- 1989
By Barton, Cattell & Curran

In this booklet statements are related to mental conditions and feelings of people at one or the other moments. Every person has got different opinions to these questions should be answered on the basis of the feelings that arises in the mind of the reader when they go through these questions.

Please mark the answer on the given paper. In every question four options are given as 'a', 'b', 'c' or 'd'. Choose one of the options which reflect your feelings at that moment. After choosing, tick (Ö) the correct answer. Please check that the serial number of the statement given in question booklet corresponds with that of the answer booklet.

e.g. (1) I am happy.

(a) Always agree

(b) Agree

(c) Disagree

(d) Always disagree.

You have to choose one of the answers. If at this moment you are feeling happy then you'll choose 'a' and mark it tick with a symbol of (Ö). Choice 'b' and 'c' represents normal happiness or unhappiness. 'b' and 'c' choice should not be used until that time when you feel incapable to check between 'a' and 'd'. Keep following instructions in mind:-

1. Do not take much time to think. At this moment what you are feeling should be immediately indicated.

2. Check that the serial number of statements in question booklet is similar to that of the answer booklet.
3. Your answer would be kept secret. Every answer should be replied whether in your view the answer that statement is not applicable on you.
4. Whatever is there in your feeling and thought that should be written in answer with full honesty.
5. Answer the questions on the basis of your present mental condition or situation.

1. At this moment I have neither any problem nor any tension:-

   a) Always Agree

   b) Agree

   c) Disagree

   d) Always Disagree.

2. At this moment there is ....on me.

   a) More pressure

   b) Some pressure

   c) Hardly any pressure

   d) No pressure.

3. At this moment I am excited

   a) Always Agree

   b) Agree

c) Disagree

d) Always Disagree.

4. The manner in which I am feeling now makes any difficult problem.............?

   a) Always challenging

   b) Challenging

   c) Full of mischief

   d) Difficult in solving.

5. At this moment I am feeling lethargic

   a) Always Agree

   b) Agree

   c) Disagree

   d) Always Disagree.

6. I am not much tired and worried that my hands are shivering.

   a) Always Agree

   b) Agree

   c) Disagree

   d) Always Disagree.

7. When I talked to people, then I thought that do they in reality take interest in what I am doing.

   a) Always Agree

   b) Agree

   c) Disagree

   d) Always Disagree.

8. Today I am continuously inspired by ideal thoughts

   a) Always Agree

   b) Agree

   c) Disagree

   d) Always Disagree.

9. I am feeling tensed and worried

   a) Always Agree

   b) Agree

   c) Disagree

   d) Always Disagree.

10. Today I am performing in my utmost ability

    a) Always Agree

    b) Agree

    c) Disagree

    d) Always Disagree.

11. The manner in which I am feeling now it appears that I am not dependable on the sympathy of the people whom I know.

    a) Always Agree

    b) Agree

    c) Disagree

    d) Always Disagree.

12. According to my present mental situation I find myself active

    a) More careful and knowingly

    b) Far more alert and careful

c) Far more excited.

d) Without thinking and understanding

13. I am feeling

a) Always aware

b) Aware

c) Lethargic

d) Always Lethargic.

14. I am not suffering from any pain or trouble which I cannot describe

a) Always aware

b) Aware

c) Lethargic

d) Always Lethargic.

15. At present I am feeling

a) Always Talkative

b) Talkative

c) Calm

d) Always calm.

16. I feel the need for sleeping but when I retire to bed than all my effort made for sleeping are in vain

a) Always Agree

b) Agree

c) Disagree

d) Always Disagree.

17. I'll feel neither stimulated nor distracted if any accident takes place

a) Always Agree

b) Agree

c) Disagree

d) Always Disagree.

18. Present conditions do not give me permission to lead easy going life

a) Always Agree

b) Agree

c) Disagree

d) Always Disagree.

19. At present I am not that much optimistic as usually I am

a) Always Agree

b) Agree

c) Disagree

d) Always Disagree.

20. If I have to take part in collective work than I will help

a) With full zeal and co-operation

b) With for more co-operation

c) With far more co-operation

d) With more co-operation.

21. Today I am much tired

a) Always Agree

b) Agree

c) Disagree

d) Always Disagree.

22. The manner in which I am feeling now I wonder that in reality I have been useful for other persons in my life

    a) Always Agree

    b) Agree

    c) Disagree

    d) Always Disagree.

23. When I am in a crowd, I feel

    a) Always Comfortable

    b) More comfortable

    c) More painful

    d) Always painful.

24. Now I prefer to hear light and soft music instead of fast loud noisy music

    a) Always Agree

    b) Agree

    c) Disagree

    d) Always Disagree.

25. At this moment I am not feeling any type of physical restlessness like indigestion, blood pressure etc.

    a) Always Agree

    b) Agree

    c) Disagree

    d) Always Disagree.

26. My life could be described as ....

    a) Always restlessness (agile) and powerless (flaccid)

    b) More powerless

c) More comfortable

d) Fully or wholly comfortable.

27. I am in a situation where I can enjoy any sort of game or sport with any friends

a) Always Agree

b) Agree

c) Disagree

d) Always Disagree.

28. Today there is continuous flow of sound waves in my mind and they create obstruction in my thoughts though I do not want any interruption in my thoughts

a) Always Agree

b) Agree

c) Disagree

d) Always Disagree.

29. I am feeling wholly spirited and powerful

a) Always Agree

b) Agree

c) Disagree

d) Always Disagree.

30. At this moment I feel that I am suffering from some flow in me

a) Always Agree

b) Agree

c) Disagree

d) Always Disagree.

31. At this moment I would like to be in the company of noisy group

    a) Always Agree

    b) Agree

    c) Disagree

    d) Always Disagree.

32. Today I have to work hard in order to remain fully aware and alert

    a) Always Agree

    b) Agree

    c) Disagree

    d) Always Disagree.

33. According to my present mental condition I fear that I may lose control or may say something ill to others

    a) Always Agree

    b) Agree

    c) Disagree

    d) Always Disagree.

34. I want to tell that at this time I am ....

    a) Fully peaceful or calm

    b) Little calm

    c) Somewhat worried

    d) Always Worried.

35. Today I have derived much pleasure by performing work for my own self

    a) Always Agree

b) Agree

c) Disagree

d) Always Disagree.

36. I am feeling mentally and physically healthy

a) Always Agree

b) Agree

c) Disagree

d) Always Disagree.

37. If in reality I had to do dome difficult task then also I would not had feel powerless and tired

a) Always Agree

b) Agree

c) Disagree

d) Always Disagree.

38. I feel that I preformed my duties in such a way that it is supported by everybody

a) Always Agree

b) Agree

c) Disagree

d) Always Disagree.

39. At this moment I am feeling more confident and brave

a) Always Agree

b) Agree

c) Disagree

d) Always Disagree.

40. At this moment it appears to me that I am clearly unable to think

    a) Always Agree

    b) Agree

    c) Disagree

    d) Always Disagree.

41. The manner in which I am feeling it appears that I will be able to control maximum occurring incidents

    a) Always Agree

    b) Agree

    c) Disagree

    d) Always Disagree.

42. At this moment I am not feeling any kind of more pressure or tension

    a) Always Agree

    b) Agree

    c) Disagree

    d) Always Disagree.

43. Loud noise and sound feel painful and uncontrollable for me

    a) Always Agree

    b) Agree

    c) Disagree

    d) Always Disagree.

44. Today when I am completely thinking about many things at that time old scenes originate in my mind

a) Always Agree

b) Agree

c) Disagree

d) Always Disagree.

45. At this moment I am feeling so much heaviness in my body that it is becoming difficult for me to move

a) Always Agree

b) Agree

c) Disagree

d) Always Disagree.

46. Today my mental situation is full of demands and complaints

a) Always Agree

b) Agree

c) Disagree

d) Always Disagree.

47. Nowadays I derive more pleasure from reading stories than from hearing them

a) Always Agree

b) Agree

c) Disagree

d) Always Disagree.

48. At this moment I can hear comparatively more clearly

a) Always Agree

b) Agree

c) Disagree

d) Always Disagree.

49. In my present mental state it appears that if my work goes wrong that I have only to shed tears

a) Always Agree

b) Agree

c) Disagree

d) Always Disagree.

50. It appears that I am inspired to do some work and there are thousands of such works which I should do.

a) Always Agree

b) Agree

c) Disagree

d) Always Disagree.

51. At that moment I am not so much happy as I find others all around me

a) Always Agree

b) Agree

c) Disagree

d) Always Disagree.

52. In my present mental state I can take an oath to do any work easily

a) Always Agree

b) Agree

c) Disagree

d) Always Disagree.

53. At this moment I feel that

a) Lie down and take rest

b) To take anything easily

c) To do something but not actively

d) To do actively and excitedly.

54. Today if I keep myself awake and think about the results of that work which I have done wrong

a) Always Agree

b) Agree

c) Disagree

d) Always Disagree.

55. If I have to talk to the other person right now then

a) This moment of thinking would be difficult for me

b) Thinking would be painful

c) There would be no pain in thinking

d) There would be ore to tell in comparison to the available time.

56. At this moment the thoughts easily creep into my mind

a) Always Agree

b) Agree

c) Disagree

d) Always Disagree.

57. At this moment I am worried that I want something but I do not know what I want

a) Always Agree

b) Agree

c) Disagree

d) Always Disagree.

58. My social life is ....

a) Not at all (without existence)

b) Little Slow

c) More Active

d) Always Active and fast.

59. In present mental state it is difficult for me to keep any important thing in my mind

a) Always Agree

b) Agree

c) Disagree

d) Always Disagree.

60. Today when I want to tell something I find difficulty in organizing my thoughts

a) Always Agree

b) Agree

c) Disagree

d) Always Disagree.

61. Right now immediately short effort would provide.........

a) In reality strength

b) Little Strength

c) Little tiredness

d) In reality tiredness.

62. Right now I am satisfied by my behavior

a) Always Agree

b) Agree

c) Disagree

d) Always Disagree.

63. If any cultural programme is being held right now then I would prefer to sit at the back and watch it

a) Always Agree

b) Agree

c) Disagree

d) Always Disagree.

64. In comparison to morning my mind is more active at this moment

a) Always Agree

b) Agree

c) Disagree

d) Always Disagree.

65. At present I am feeling comfortable

a) Always Agree

b) Agree

c) Disagree

d) Always Disagree.

66. In present mental state I can get pleasure from games only when I would win

a) Always Agree

b) Agree

c) Disagree

d) Always Disagree.

67. At present I feel that every work of my life would be as I want it to be

    a) Always Agree

    b) Agree

    c) Disagree

    d) Always Disagree.

68. If I do effort to do fully physically work that I would feel giddiness and unconsciousness

    a) Always Agree

    b) Agree

    c) Disagree

    d) Always Disagree.

69. At this moment my desire to do work is equivalent to my normal level

    a) Always Agree

    b) Agree

    c) Disagree

    d) Always Disagree.

70. At this moment I am being sad by thinking about bad thoughts which I have done and I am being overweighed by these thoughts

    a) Always Agree

    b) Agree

    c) Disagree

    d) Always Disagree.

71. If I am being called right now to speak among large number of audience (listeners) then I

    a) Would be ineffectual or feeble and loose my confidence

    b) Little feeble

    c) Much peaceful and confident

    d) Always peaceful and confident..

72. Today thoughts are coming slowly

    a) Always Agree

    b) Agree

    c) Disagree

    d) Always Disagree.

73. I am in good and happy mood

    a) Always Agree

    b) Agree

    c) Disagree

    d) Always Disagree.

74. Today more expectations are there

    a) Always Agree

    b) Agree

    c) Disagree

    d) Always Disagree.

75. Today I feel that whatever I do, I would be better in comparison to the past

    a) Always Agree

    b) Agree

c) Disagree

d) Always Disagree.

76. I want my life should not be more hard and doubtful or uncertain as it is now

    a) Always Agree

    b) Agree

    c) Disagree

    d) Always Disagree.

77. I feel that I am suffering from fatigue (tiredness) and I am powerless

    a) Always Agree

    b) Agree

    c) Disagree

    d) Always Disagree.

78. I am completely satisfied by my own self

    a) Always Agree

    b) Agree

    c) Disagree

    d) Always Disagree.

79. In comparison to past today I feel that many people estimate that I am...........

    a) Always Calm

    b) Less Calm

    c) Less Active

    d) Always Active.

80. It appears that time is passing very slowly

a) Always Agree

b) Agree

c) Disagree

d) Always Disagree.

81. Today I am finding myself unaccepted, tired and irritated

a) Always Agree

b) Agree

c) Disagree

d) Always Disagree.

82. At present I feel that I am performing ....level of work

a) High

b) Average

c) Bellow Average

d) Very Low.

83. I am feeling so much powerless that I wonder how I would spend my whole day

a) Always Agree

b) Agree

c) Disagree

d) Always Disagree.

84. At this moment I have got feel that I am prepared for any unexpected situation

a) Always Agree

b) Agree

c) Disagree

d) Always Disagree.

85. At this moment I have got enough strength to go to far off place

a) Always Agree

b) Agree

c) Disagree

d) Always Disagree.

86. I feel that today when I'll go to sleep then I would have no problem

a) Always Agree

b) Agree

c) Disagree

d) Always Disagree.

87. At present I am fully satisfied with my physical attraction (Fitness)

a) Always Agree

b) Agree

c) Disagree

d) Always Disagree.

88. The manner in which I am feeling now on that basis I can get pleasure from all the things

a) Always Agree

b) Agree

c) Disagree

d) Always Disagree.

89. At this moment I am more worried
    a) Always Agree
    b) Agree
    c) Disagree
    d) Always Disagree.
90. Today I am feeling
    a) Without Anger
    b) Little bit anger
    c) Somewhat anger
    d) More anger.
91. I am in excited (delighted) state
    a) Always Agree
    b) Agree
    c) Disagree
    d) Always Disagree.
92. At present moment it is difficult for me to tell anyone about my present dream
    a) Always Agree
    b) Agree
    c) Disagree
    d) Always Disagree.
93. Physically I feel............
    a) Fully tired
    b) Tired
    c) Powerful

d) Fully Powerful.

94. At this moment whatever happened I am satisfied with it

a) Always Agree

b) Agree

c) Disagree

d) Always Disagree.

95. Today when I talk, I can include other people also in my happiness

a) Always Agree

b) Agree

c) Disagree

d) Always Disagree.

96. It appears that many things are happening together

a) Always Agree

b) Agree

c) Disagree

d) Always Disagree.

APPENDIX-B

SCORE SHEET FOR EIGHT STATE QUETIONNAIRE [8SQ]

NAME OF ATHLETE :
NAME OF GAME :
LEVEL OF PARTICIPATION : DISTRICT / STATE / NATIONAL / INTERNATIONAL

Remember to answer according to the mood you are in ***RIGHT NOW***	
Example : I feel in a happy mood a) very true b) fairly true c) fairly false d) very false a b c d ○ ○ ○ ○	• Use pencil only. • Be sure each mark is black and fills the entire space. • Erase completely any answer you wish to change.

1	a b c d ○ ○ ○ ○	2	a b c d ○ ○ ○ ○	3	a b c d ○ ○ ○ ○	4	a b c d ○ ○ ○ ○	5	a b c d ○ ○ ○ ○	6	a b c d ○ ○ ○ ○	7	a b c d ○ ○ ○ ○	8	a b c d ○ ○ ○ ○
9	a b c d ○ ○ ○ ○	10	a b c d ○ ○ ○ ○	11	a b c d ○ ○ ○ ○	12	a b c d ○ ○ ○ ○	13	a b c d ○ ○ ○ ○	14	a b c d ○ ○ ○ ○	15	a b c d ○ ○ ○ ○	16	a b c d ○ ○ ○ ○

(Contd...)

17	a b c d	18	a b c d	19	a b c d	20	a b c d	21	a b c d	22	a b c d	23	a b c d	24	a b c d
25	a b c d	26	a b c d	27	a b c d	28	a b c d	29	a b c d	30	a b c d	31	a b c d	32	a b c d
33	a b c d	34	a b c d	35	a b c d	36	a b c d	37	a b c d	38	a b c d	39	a b c d	40	a b c d
41	a b c d	42	a b c d	43	a b c d	44	a b c d	45	a b c d	46	a b c d	47	a b c d	48	a b c d
49	a b c d	50	a b c d	51	a b c d	52	a b c d	53	a b c d	54	a b c d	55	a b c d	56	a b c d
57	a b c d	58	a b c d	59	a b c d	60	a b c d	61	a b c d	62	a b c d	63	a b c d	64	a b c d
65	a b c d	66	a b c d	67	a b c d	68	a b c d	69	a b c d	70	a b c d	71	a b c d	72	a b c d
73	a b c d	74	a b c d	75	a b c d	76	a b c d	77	a b c d	78	a b c d	79	a b c d	80	a b c d
81	a b c d	82	a b c d	83	a b c d	84	a b c d	85	a b c d	86	a b c d	87	a b c d	88	a b c d
89	a b c d	90	a b c d	91	a b c d	92	a b c d	93	a b c d	94	a b c d	95	a b c d	96	a b c d

Ax	St	De	Rg	Fg	Gt	Ex	Ar

APPENDIX - C

Scores of Eight State Questionnair [8sq]

FENCING

Sl. No.	*Anxiety*	*Stress*	*Depression*	*Regression*	*Fatigue*	*Guilt*	*Extraversion*	*Arousal*	*Level*
1	*2*	*3*	*4*	*5*	*6*	*7*	*8*	*9*	*10*
1.	12	13	12	12	16	14	15	12	District
2.	14	14	16	19	16	14	15	11	District
3.	18	11	10	15	17	18	19	12	District
4.	13	18	17	12	15	14	15	16	District
5.	8	10	16	14	17	17	19	14	District
6.	17	14	13	18	18	14	13	14	District
7.	17	12	19	13	17	12	22	14	District
8.	15	12	13	13	15	12	20	14	District
9.	13	14	18	18	19	15	15	16	District
10.	19	18	17	13	21	16	14	15	District

(Contd...)

1	*2*	*3*	*4*	*5*	*6*	*7*	*8*	*9*	*10*
11.	16	13	12	12	17	13	14	12	State
12.	14	12	12	11	14	11	10	14	State
13.	17	15	12	10	14	14	16	14	State
14.	14	18	11	16	15	11	15	14	State
15.	18	10	14	16	16	15	17	12	State
16.	15	15	13	13	17	18	14	14	State
17.	11	11	12	10	15	11	15	15	State
18.	17	13	12	14	19	12	16	16	State
19.	16	11	12	11	12	13	17	15	State
20.	19	15	11	14	15	13	15	12	State
21.	17	14	17	13	18	14	17	12	National
22.	16	14	16	14	18	14	19	13	National
23.	15	10	15	12	14	14	17	13	National
24.	16	16	16	14	18	16	16	14	National

(Contd...)

1	2	3	4	5	6	7	8	9	10
25.	15	15	15	14	18	17	17	15	National
26.	17	6	18	18	16	13	15	11	National
27.	14	13	13	13	16	12	18	15	National
28.	16	9	17	10	17	12	19	13	National
29.	16	14	14	14	18	12	17	14	National
30.	16	13	16	14	16	15	15	12	National
31.	16	12	17	14	19	12	19	11	International
32.	16	14	16	12	15	16	17	15	International
33.	16	13	16	13	18	15	19	12	International
34.	16	15	11	13	13	17	18	13	International
35.	18	13	12	16	14	16	18	16	International
36.	16	11	15	15	19	12	18	14	International
37.	16	12	16	13	18	13	17	13	International
38.	16	9	16	14	18	13	21	14	International

(Contd...)

1	*2*	*3*	*4*	*5*	*6*	*7*	*8*	*9*	*10*
39.	16	10	13	11	19	17	16	10	International
40.	15	15	13	11	14	18	19	16	International
SOCCER									
41.	13	12	15	15	17	14	18	15	District
42.	9	7	3	9	11	10	9	5	District
43.	12	14	10	11	9	12	17	11	District
44.	6	9	16	7	15	13	13	9	District
45.	15	11	14	14	15	17	17	17	District
46.	11	11	14	17	13	17	17	11	District
47.	12	15	19	17	17	14	20	19	District
48.	13	14	11	12	14	12	16	15	District
49.	11	24	13	16	11	10	16	14	District
50.	15	14	10	12	15	13	19	14	District
51.	18	13	15	13	11	13	13	12	State

(Contd...)

1	2	3	4	5	6	7	8	9	10
52.	18	15	16	15	14	14	14	16	State
53.	12	12	15	15	19	15	14	16	State
54.	13	9	15	12	19	17	19	9	State
55.	13	11	15	14	17	15	16	13	State
56.	22	12	20	19	20	20	23	13	State
57.	16	14	13	18	17	15	16	21	State
58.	14	13	20	14	20	17	24	22	State
59.	20	16	13	18	14	17	18	13	State
60.	16	12	20	17	20	12	12	22	State
61.	18	13	16	17	14	13	14	17	National
62.	18	14	16	15	15	15	14	15	National
63.	19	15	18	17	15	14	14	19	National
64.	18	13	17	14	16	14	14	15	National
65.	18	14	15	16	15	14	14	17	National

(Contd...)

1	2	3	4	5	6	7	8	9	10
66.	17	14	16	17	16	14	14	17	National
67.	18	12	15	16	15	14	14	18	National
68.	17	11	17	12	14	16	15	11	National
69.	13	12	16	10	15	13	17	13	National
70.	17	14	13	14	18	15	19	14	National
71.	17	11	15	13	18	16	19	13	International
72.	16	12	14	13	19	12	20	12	International
73.	16	16	16	17	22	16	26	12	International
74.	16	11	15	15	17	12	16	10	International
75.	18	13	18	11	15	20	19	11	International
76.	18	15	16	16	15	15	14	17	International
77.	17	11	12	10	15	11	15	15	International
78.	17	15	16	12	15	14	15	16	International
79.	18	14	16	14	16	14	14	15	International

(Contd...)

1	*2*	*3*	*4*	*5*	*6*	*7*	*8*	*9*	*10*
80.	17	14	15	12	14	13	12	17	International
TAEKWONDO									
81.	17	14	16	12	15	14	14	12	District
82.	15	14	13	14	17	12	16	14	District
83..	18	17	12	13	13	14	19	14	District
84.	12	11	12	8	16	15	10	13	District
85.	16	14	17	13	17	15	15	17	District
86.	21	17	14	16	19	13	10	17	District
87.	15	15	16	16	21	17	15	16	District
88.	18	14	14	8	12	13	17	15	District
89.	17	14	12	13	18	13	18	14	District
90.	17	16	15	12	16	14	17	15	District
91.	17	18	15	17	20	15	21	17	State
92.	22	12	16	14	15	19	16	12	State

(Contd...)

1	2	3	4	5	6	7	8	9	10
93.	20	15	21	15	16	13	20	18	State
94.	18	20	16	16	19	16	20	18	State
95.	18	10	12	16	20	16	22	13	State
96.	15	15	16	19	16	19	16	14	State
97.	16	18	20	13	17	18	14	16	State
98.	18	14	19	12	25	12	18	16	State
99.	19	14	12	14	18	16	18	19	State
100.	18	13	16	18	16	16	26	19	State
101.	16	11	17	12	15	16	16	12	National
102.	17	13	16	12	16	14	18	13	National
103.	15	12	13	14	16	16	15	15	National
104.	13	8	13	14	15	11	18	11	National
105.	17	15	16	11	15	13	17	14	National
106.	17	12	19	13	15	14	18	12	National

(Contd...)

1	*2*	*3*	*4*	*5*	*6*	*7*	*8*	*9*	*10*
107.	16	10	17	12	16	13	17	12	National
108.	18	15	14	14	17	14	17	16	National
109.	16	17	14	14	14	14	19	12	National
110.	16	12	15	15	19	15	18	12	National
111.	17	14	16	12	15	14	14	12	International
112.	15	14	13	14	17	12	16	14	International
113.	18	17	12	13	13	14	19	14	International
114.	12	11	12	8	16	15	10	13	International
115.	16	14	17	13	17	15	15	17	International
116.	21	17	14	16	19	13	10	17	International
117.	15	15	16	16	21	17	15	16	International
118.	18	14	14	8	12	13	17	15	International
119.	17	14	12	13	18	13	18	14	International
120.	17	16	15	12	16	14	17	15	International

(Contd...)

1	*2*	*3*	*4*	*5*	*6*	*7*	*8*	*9*	*10*
JUDO									
121.	11	9	13	14	15	13	10	12	District
122.	13	14	14	14	16	16	12	13	District
123.	14	14	16	22	18	13	19	14	District
124.	14	13	15	19	20	14	20	16	District
125.	16	9	18	13	18	17	17	13	District
126.	15	12	17	9	16	12	18	14	District
127.	15	14	14	14	14	13	14	15	District
128.	13	16	15	18	17	14	18	14	District
129.	14	13	16	14	16	13	16	13	District
130.	19	16	14	17	18	17	15	13	District
131.	16	12	11	10	17	14	13	13	State
132.	16	12	13	13	16	13	15	14	State
133.	12	16	11	13	12	14	15	17	State

(Contd...)

1	2	3	4	5	6	7	8	9	10
134.	15	14	14	14	13	10	15	15	State
135.	13	11	11	11	20	16	26	12	State
136.	14	18	14	14	20	17	19	15	State
137.	18	18	11	18	17	21	21	15	State
138.	14	14	12	11	17	16	17	14	State
139.	13	16	15	11	17	16	14	16	State
140.	17	12	14	15	16	11	14	15	State
141.	16	10	16	11	15	15	18	12	National
142.	17	9	13	15	17	12	16	11	National
143.	18	7	16	10	16	11	19	14	National
144.	15	14	18	16	19	16	14	12	National
145.	17	9	17	12	14	16	13	12	National
146.	19	15	17	14	22	16	17	14	National
147.	18	17	19	15	16	15	20	12	National

(Contd...)

1	2	3	4	5	6	7	8	9	10
148.	19	13	14	15	18	14	19	15	National
149.	15	13	16	17	16	17	16	15	National
150.	16	18	14	19	17	17	18	17	National
151.	17	11	14	11	16	15	12	13	International
152.	18	11	16	11	15	15	16	12	International
153.	15	17	15	14	15	10	11	16	International
154.	18	14	14	13	18	13	16	15	International
155.	15	15	13	15	17	10	14	14	International
156.	15	16	16	12	21	13	16	13	International
157.	16	16	12	10	13	13	17	14	International
158.	17	14	15	14	16	12	12	15	International
159.	17	18	15	14	12	17	13	16	International
160.	17	13	16	13	17	16	18	17	International

(Contd...)

1	2	3	4	5	6	7	8	9	10
SAPAK-TAKRAW									
161.	13	17	12	13	17	14	16	13	District
162.	15	12	15	11	15	13	20	15	District
163.	15	12	13	18	18	16	19	13	District
164.	14	12	17	14	17	13	19	15	District
165.	16	14	16	12	18	15	16	15	District
166.	18	14	16	17	18	13	20	15	District
167.	17	14	14	21	14	18	20	13	District
168.	17	13	15	14	18	14	14	16	District
169.	17	17	13	11	19	13	18	16	District
170.	13	15	16	15	18	13	13	11	District
171.	18	17	21	17	18	17	20	15	State
172.	16	19	14	13	19	11	20	14	State
173.	16	14	13	13	19	19	16	14	State

(Contd...)

1	2	3	4	5	6	7	8	9	10
174.	15	14	15	17	18	16	16	14	State
175.	18	13	16	15	19	16	16	18	State
176.	17	15	15	19	13	16	24	19	State
177.	15	16	17	14	17	15	15	17	State
178.	15	17	14	16	19	14	23	17	State
179.	16	15	17	17	20	14	20	20	State
180.	20	13	15	12	17	18	20	16	State
181.	15	13	17	12	16	14	18	13	National
182.	15	9	16	13	16	13	16	15	National
183.	16	15	18	13	18	16	18	12	National
184.	15	14	15	14	18	14	14	13	National
185.	17	9	18	17	19	14	20	15	National
186.	14	11	16	12	18	16	15	12	National
187.	16	13	16	12	16	13	17	15	National

(Contd...)

1	*2*	*3*	*4*	*5*	*6*	*7*	*8*	*9*	*10*
188.	16	12	15	15	14	13	22	14	National
189.	17	10	14	12	16	15	16	14	National
190.	17	12	17	11	18	13	17	12	National
191	19	14	16	12	17	13	15	13	International
192.	19	15	16	12	16	14	19	14	International
193.	17	12	15	11	14	12	17	15	International
194.	19	14	15	9	16	14	13	15	International
195.	15	12	13	14	18	12	17	17	International
196.	16	10	13	16	18	14	18	12	International
197.	10	11	12	11	12	15	15	16	International
198.	16	16	15	13	18	14	16	12	International
199.	20	11	14	18	14	10	16	14	International
200.	19	12	18	13	17	13	16	17	International

APPENDIX - D

SCORES OF AAPHER YOUTH FITNESS TEST

FENCING

Sl. No.	Pull-Up	Bent KneeSit - Up	Standing Broad Jump	Shuttle Run	50 M. Dash	800 M.	Height	Weight	Level
1	*2*	*3*	*4*	*5*	*6*	*7*	*8*	*9*	*10*
1.	14 count	30 count/min.	2.17 mts.	10.16 sec.	7.85 sec.	3240 mts.	173 cm.	58 kg.	District
2.	9 count	48 count/min.	1.75 mts.	10 sec.	7.89 sec.	2800 mts.	168 cm.	57 kg.	District
3.	14 count	49 count/min.	2.22 mts.	10.6 sec.	7.67 sec.	3200 mts.	168 cm.	56 kg.	District
4.	9 count	46 count/min.	2.22 mts.	10.14 sec.	7.60 sec.	2800 mts.	165 cm.	56 kg.	District
5.	9 count	32 count/min.	1.54 mts.	12.7 sec.	11.50 sec.	2100 mts.	163 cm.	45 kg.	District
6.	12 count	43 count/min.	1.55 mts.	11.39 sec.	9.36 sec.	2300 mts.	158 cm.	50 kg.	District
7.	10 count.	40 count/min.	1.71 mts.	10 sec.	9.95 sec.	2380 mts.	153 cm.	45 kg.	District
8.	11 count	40 count/min.	1.68 mts.	10.10 sec.	9.40 sec.	2150 mts.	158 cm.	40 kg.	District
10.	11 count	45 count/min.	2.10 mts.	10 sec.	7.80 sec.	2250 mts.	168 cm.	56 kg.	District

(Contd...)

1	2	3	4	5	6	7	8	9	10
11.	13 count	53 count/min.	2.31 mts.	9.47 sec.	7.35 sec.	3100 mts.	170 cm.	57 kg.	State
12.	10 count	49 count/min.	1.94 mts.	10.7 sec.	7.94 sec.	3080 mts.	163 cm.	52 kg.	State
13.	9 count	42 count/min.	2.5 mts.	10.46 sec.	8.36 sec.	2920 mts.	170 cm.	55 kg.	State
14.	11 count	42 count/min.	1.91 mts.	11.9 sec.	8.99 sec.	2400 mts.	168 cm.	49 kg.	State
15.	14 count	40 count/min.	1.83 mts.	10.72 sec.	8.70 sec.	2600 mts.	160 cm.	50 kg.	State
16.	12 count	35 count/min.	1.66 mts.	11.29 sec.	8.84 sec.	2400mts.	160 cm.	49 kg.	State
17.	12 count	38 count/min.	1.79 mts.	11.13 sec.	9.25 sec.	2490mts.	157 cm.	48 kg.	State
18.	11 count	49 count/min.	2.10 mts.	10.10 sec.	7.95 sec.	3065 mts.	168 cm.	55 kg.	State
19.	12 count	50 count/min.	1.98 mts.	10 sec.	7.80 sec.	3060 mts.	163 cm.	52 kg.	State
20.	15 count	37 count/min.	1.71 mts.	10.90 sec.	8.80 sec.	2460 mts.	153 cm.	45 kg.	State
21.	15count	52count/min	2.34mts	9.77sec.	6.95 sec.	3320 mts.	165 cm.	55 kg.	National
22.	9 count	38 count/min.	2.22 mts.	10.8 sec.	7.60 sec.	2700 mts.	168 cm.	56 kg.	National
23.	12 count	count/min 42.	2.42 mts.	9.79 sec.	7.96 sec.	2800 mts.	173 cm.	56 kg.	National
24.	18 count.	50 count/min.	1.78 mts.	9.52 sec.	7.30 sec.	2400 mts.	163 cm.	50 kg.	National

(Contd...)

1	*2*	*3*	*4*	*5*	*6*	*7*	*8*	*9*	*10*
25.	15 count.	39 count/min.	2.13 mts.	10.50 sec.	7.80 sec.	2480 mts.	165 cm.	50 kg.	National
26.	14 count.	31 count/min.	1.82 mts.	10.94 sec.	8.95 sec.	2400 mts.	163 cm.	45 kg.	National
27.	17 count.	42 count/min.	1.83 mts.	11.1 sec.	8.60 sec.	2380 mts.	165 cm.	52 kg.	National
28.	16 count.	32 count/min.	1.84 mts.	10 sec.	7.35 sec.	2380 mts.	165 cm.	45 kg.	National
29.	12 count.	38 count/min.	1.72 mts.	11.3 sec.	8.23 sec.	2390 mts.	163 cm.	48 kg.	National
30.	13 count	48 count/min.	2.28 mts.	9.90 sec.	7.90 sec.	2750 mts.	160 cm.	45 kg.	National
31.	16 count	57 count/min.	2.55 mts.	8.45 sec.	6.06 sec.	3950 mts.	168 cm.	65 kg.	International
32.	12 count	60 count/min.	2.55 mts.	8.10 sec.	5.92 sec.	3890 mts.	167 cm.	62 kg.	International
33.	16 count	59 count/min.	2.55 mts.	7.98 sec.	5.65 sec.	3310 mts.	165 cm.	55 kg.	International
34.	10 count	59 count/min.	2.53 mts.	8.32 sec.	6.04 sec.	3416 mts.	171 cm.	69 kg.	International
35.	22 count.	48 count/min.	2.20 mts.	8.92 sec.	6.96 sec.	3037 mts.	163 cm.	54 kg.	International
36.	24 count.	45 count/min.	2.17 mts.	8.98 sec.	7.01 sec.	3050 mts.	163 cm.	54 kg.	International
37.	15 count.	41 count/min.	2.40 mts.	8.60 sec.	6.80 sec.	3100 mts.	163 cm.	53 kg.	International
38.	21 count	43 count/min.	2.45 mts.	8.55 sec.	6.75 sec.	3200 mts.	158 cm.	51 kg.	International

(Contd...)

1	2	3	4	5	6	7	8	9	10
39.	22 count.	46 count/min.	2.50 mts.	8.52 sec.	6.78 sec.	3020 mts.	160 cm.	52 kg.	International
40.	20 count	48 count/min.	2.53 mts.	8.50 sec.	6.70 sec.	3150 mts.	160 cm.	53 kg.	International
SOCCER									
41.	8 count	35 count/min.	2.30 mts.	9.32 sec.	7.40 sec.	3478 mts.	163 cm.	40 kg.	District
42.	9 count	43 count/min.	2.21 mts.	9.20 sec.	7.45 sec.	3453 mts.	163 cm.	50 kg.	District
43.	10 count	44 count/min.	2.28 mts.	9.41 sec.	6.95 sec.	3678 mts.	160 cm.	50 kg.	District
44.	7count	27 count/min.	2.41 mts.	8.83 sec.	7.05 sec.	3650 mts.	163 cm.	50 kg.	District
45.	6 count	23 count/min.	2.56 mts.	9.42 sec.	6.92 sec.	3453 mts.	163 cm.	53 kg.	District
46.	7 count	32 count/min.	2.51 mts.	9.20 sec.	7.30 sec.	3475 mts.	165 cm.	52kg.	District
47.	8 count	36 count/min.	2.36 mts.	9.00 sec.	7.11 sec.	3582 mts.	160 cm.	50 kg.	District
48.	7 count	33 count/min.	2.34 mts.	9.32 sec.	7.37 sec.	3470 mts.	162 cm.	51 kg.	District
49.	7 count	33 count/min.	2.44 mts.	8.78 sec.	6.98 sec.	3678 mts.	167 cm.	55 kg.	District
50.	6 count	28 count/min.	2.36 mts.	8.88 sec.	7.06 sec.	3555 mts.	163 cm.	44 kg.	District
51.	10 count	60 count/min.	2.35 mts.	8.70 sec.	6.20 sec.	3645 mts.	163 cm.	59 kg.	State

(Contd...)

1	*2*	*3*	*4*	*5*	*6*	*7*	*8*	*9*	*10*
52.	13 count	58 count/min.	2.32 mts.	8.72 sec.	6.23 sec.	3630 mts.	165 cm.	57 kg.	State
53.	9 count	57 count/min.	2.29 mts.	8.81 sec.	6.30 sec.	3625 mts.	165 cm.	57 kg.	State
54.	12 count	58 count/min.	2.37 mts.	8.75 sec.	6.25 sec.	3610 mts.	168 cm.	58 kg.	State
55.	13 count	61 count/min.	2.39 mts.	8.73 sec.	6.21 sec.	3650 mts.	165 cm.	57 kg.	State
56.	14 count	60 count/min.	2.37 mts.	8.72 sec.	6.10 sec.	3590 mts.	170 cm.	55 kg.	State
57.	13 count	59 count/min.	2.33 mts.	8.79 sec.	6.22 sec.	3550 mts.	158 cm.	54 kg.	State
58.	12 count	58 count/min.	2.34 mts.	8.77 sec.	6.19 sec.	3620 mts.	165 cm.	59kg.	State
59.	15 count	59 count/min.	2.31 mts	8.71 sec.	6.16 sec.	3600 mts.	160 cm.	56 kg.	State
60.	14 count	59 count/min.	2.30 mts.	8.73 sec.	6.26 sec.	3580 mts.	168 cm.	62 kg.	State
61.	8 count	58 count/min.	2.10 mts.	8.60 sec.	6.20 sec.	3690 mts.	165 cm.	56 kg.	National
62.	9 count	50 count/min.	2.15 mts.	8.92 sec.	6.59 sec.	3700 mts.	163 cm.	61 kg.	National
63.	15 count	58 count/min.	2.18 mts.	8.41 sec.	6.43 sec.	3750 mts.	170 cm.	62 kg.	National
64.	13 count	59count/min.	2.20 mts.	8.39 sec.	6.30 sec.	3740 mts.	170 cm.	64 kg.	National
65.	14 count	60 count/min.	2.25 mts.	8.35 sec.	6.40 sec.	3720 mts.	168 cm.	60 kg.	National

(Contd...)

1	2	3	4	5	6	7	8	9	10
66.	13 count	57 count/min.	2.19 mts.	8.40 sec.	6.37 sec.	3710 mts.	168 cm.	59 kg.	National
67.	14 count	58 count/min.	2.22 mts.	8.30 sec.	6.32 sec.	3655 mts.	165 cm.	63 kg.	National
68.	15 count	60 count/min.	2.31 mts.	8.25 sec.	6.20 sec.	3600 mts.	165 cm.	62 kg.	National
69.	23 count.	47 count/min.	1.79 mts.	10.24 sec.	8.50 sec.	2892 mts.	155 cm.	49 kg.	National
70.	8 count.	40 count/min.	2.22 mts.	9.24 sec.	8.10 sec.	3780 mts.	160 cm.	49 kg.	National
71.	21 count.	43 count/min.	1.94 mts.	9.86 sec.	6.78 sec.	2995 mts.	157 cm.	53 kg.	International
72.	29 count.	65 count/min.	2.22 mts.	9.80 sec.	6.80 sec.	2990 mts.	165 cm.	58 kg.	International
73.	25 count.	61 count/min.	2.07 mts.	9.6 sec.	6.75 sec.	2950 mts.	163 cm.	53 kg.	International
74.	26 count.	43 count/min	2.27 mts.	9.6 sec.	6.69 sec.	3050 mts.	158 cm.	53 kg.	International
75.	22 count	65 count/min.	2.90 mts.	8.10 sec.	6.40 sec.	3990 mts.	178 cm.	65 kg.	International
76.	21 count	66 count/min.	2.78 mts.	8.15 sec.	6.39 sec.	4000 mts.	170 cm.	63 kg.	International
77.	20 count	60 count/min.	2.67 mts.	8.20 sec.	6.45 sec.	3950 mts.	173 cm.	62 kg.	International
78.	23 count	62 count/min.	2.70 mts.	8.16 sec.	6.35 sec.	3920 mts.	170 cm.	64 kg.	International
79.	24 count	63 count/min.	2.75 mts.	8.13 sec.	6.32 sec.	3980 mts.	170 cm.	61 kg.	International

(Contd...)

1	2	3	4	5	6	7	8	9	10
80.	22 count	61 count/min.	2.81 mts.	8.18 sec.	6.30 sec.	3995 mts.	168 cm.	63 kg.	International
SAPAK - TAKRAW									
81.	5 count	23 count/min.	1.65 mts.	9.10 sec.	7.13 sec.	3096 mts.	160 cm.	47 kg.	District
82.	3 count	24 count/min.	1.95 mts.	9.02 sec.	6.93 sec.	3100 mts.	170 cm.	54 kg.	District
83.	6 count	15 count/min.	1.95 mts.	9.05 sec.	6.63 sec.	3018 mts.	163 cm.	48 kg.	District
84.	12 count	44 count/min.	1.70 mts.	10.20 sec.	7.06 sec.	2400 mts.	158 cm.	45 kg.	District
85.	13 count	45 count/min.	1.69 mts.	10.15 sec.	7.15 sec.	2300 mts.	155 cm.	42 kg.	District
86.	9 count	39 count/min.	1.55 mts.	10.30 sec.	7.21 sec.	2240 mts.	160 cm.	40 kg.	District
87.	9 count	43 count/min.	1.94 mts.	9.09 sec.	6.53 sec.	3150 mts.	163 cm.	47 kg.	District
88.	10 count	42 count/min.	2.09 mts.	8.95 sec.	6.55 sec.	3050 mts.	165 cm.	50 kg.	District
89.	7 count	38 count/min.	12.10 mts.	9.99 sec.	6.62 sec.	3020 mts.	165 cm.	54 kg.	District
90.	11 count	48 count/min.	11.99 mts.	9.01 sec.	6.45 sec.	3110 mts.	170 cm.	56 kg.	District
91.	10 count	33 count/min.	2.27 mts.	8.25 sec.	6.55 sec.	3490 mts.	165 cm.	55 kg.	State
92.	6 count	41 count/min.	2.32 mts.	8.49 sec.	6.16 sec.	3490 mts.	167 cm.	54 kg.	State

(Contd...)

1	2	3	4	5	6	7	8	9	10
93.	4 count	42 count/min.	2.16 mts.	8.69 sec.	6.25 sec.	3254 mts.	157 cm.	56 kg.	State
94.	5 count	44 count/min.	1.94 mts.	8.77 sec.	6.44 sec.	3392 mts.	157 cm.	55 kg.	State
95.	8 count	42 count/min.	2.35 mts.	8.20 sec.	6.30 sec.	3310 mts.	153 cm.	50 kg.	State
96.	7 count	44 count/min.	2.40 mts.	8.15 sec.	6.20 sec.	3290 mts.	152 cm.	52 kg.	State
97.	17 count	40 count/min.	1.98 mts.	9.99 sec.	7.93 sec.	2450 mts.	160 cm.	50 kg.	State
98.	16 count	30 count/min.	1.96 mts.	10.10 sec.	8.09 sec.	2320 mts.	153 cm.	49 kg.	State
99.	14 count	33 count/min.	1.88 mts.	10.20 sec.	8.19 sec.	2390 mts.	152 cm.	45 kg.	State
100.	15 count	35 count/min.	1.91 mts.	10.25 sec.	8.31 sec.	2280 mts.	155 cm.	40 kg.	State
101.	7 count	50 count/min	2.51 mts.	8.44 sec.	6.37 sec.	3276 mts.	166 cm.	58 kg.	National
102.	9 count	45 count/min.	2.27 mts.	8.53 sec.	6.15 sec.	3189 mts.	170 cm.	63 kg.	National
103.	16 count	49 count/min.	1.94 mts.	8.31 sec.	6.13 sec.	3037 mts.	164 cm.	55 kg.	National
104.	13 count	57 count/min.	2.33 mts.	8.26 sec.	5.88 sec.	3254 mts.	178 cm.	70 kg.	National
105.	14 count	59 count/min.	2.30 mts.	8.35 sec.	6.40 sec.	3230 mts.	170 cm.	61 kg.	National
106.	15 count	60 count/min.	2.35 mts.	8.29 sec.	6.25 sec.	3260 mts.	168 cm.	57 kg.	National

(Contd...)

1	2	3	4	5	6	7	8	9	10
107.	20 count	23 count/min.	1.74 mts.	9.88 sec.	7.12 sec.	2539 mts.	155 cm.	52 kg.	National
108.	23 count	32 count/min.	1.78 mts.	9.65 sec.	7.72 sec.	2461 mts.	160 cm.	53 kg.	National
109.	22 count	34 count/min.	1.76 mts.	9.50 sec.	7.47 sec.	2412 mts.	152 cm.	54 kg.	National
110.	9 count	51 count/min.	2.10 mts.	8.50 sec.	6.20 sec.	3240 mts.	165 cm.	58 kg.	National
111.	16 count	55 count/min	2.31 mts.	8.55 sec.	6.25 sec.	3500 mts.	170 cm.	59 kg.	International
112.	15 count	57 count/min.	2.40 mts.	8.50 sec.	6.20 sec.	3450 mts.	165 cm.	56 kg.	International
113.	10 count	49 count/min.	2.35 mts.	8.98 sec.	6.30 sec.	3660 mts.	160 cm.	50 kg.	International
114.	22 count	50 count/min.	2.45 mts.	8.70 sec.	6.19 sec.	3520 mts.	166 cm.	53 kg.	International
115.	25 count	52 count/min.	2.45 mts.	8.45 sec.	6.12 sec.	3490 mts.	165 cm.	52 kg.	International
116.	18 count	54 count/min.	2.50 mts.	8.32 sec.	6.09 sec.	3470 mts.	168 cm.	55 kg.	International
117.	11 count	50 count/min.	2.25 mts.	8.95 sec.	6.35 sec.	3520 mts.	163 cm.	49 kg.	International
118.	16 count	52 count/min.	2.42 mts.	8.10 sec.	5.95 sec.	3420 mts.	168 cm.	57 kg.	International
119.	14 count	51 count/min.	2.39 mts.	8.50 sec.	6.10 sec.	3410 mts.	168 cm.	56 kg.	International
120.	19 count	50 count/min.	2.74 mts.	8.60 sec.	6.15 sec.	3460 mts.	165 cm.	54 kg.	International

(Contd...)

1	2	3	4	5	6	7	8	9	10
Taekwondo									
121.	20 count	70 count/ min	2.23mts.	8.97sec.	6.44 sec.	3254 mts.	168 cm	55 kg	District
122.	5count	45 count/ min	2.08 mts.	9.11 sec.	6.57 sec.	3130 mts.	160 cm	44 kg	District
123.	11 count	50 count/min	2.16 mts.	9.06 sec.	7.93 sec.	3416mts.	171cm	54 kg	District
124.	5 count	58 count/min	1.98mts.	9.65 sec.	7.05 sec.	3390 mts.	170 cm	56 kg	District
125.	9 count	59 count/min	2.22 mts.	9.15 sec.	6.50 sec.	3368 mts.	173 cm	53 kg.	District
126.	11count	60 count/min	2.15mts.	9.30 sec.	6.58 sec.	3270 mts.	173 cm	57 kg.	District
127.	13 count	45 count/min	1.50mts.	10.50 sec.	9.55sec.	2400mts	155cm	48kg	District
128.	13 count	52 count/min	2.10mts.	9.01 sec.	6.97 sec.	2290 mts	165 cm	56 kg.	District
129.	12 count	43 count/min	1.55mts.	10.05sec.	9.65sec.	2350mts.	150cm	44 kg	District
130.	13 count	41 count/min	1.58mts.	10.10sec.	9.70 sec.	2370 mts	158cm	55kg	District
131.	7 count	54 count/min	2.34mts	8.80sec.	6.10sec.	3692mts	170cm	60 kg	State

(Contd...)

1	2	3	4	5	6	7	8	9	10
132.	19 count	65 count/min	2.37 mts	8.70sec.	6.38sec.	4000mts.	167cm	47 kg	State
133.	10 count	68 count/min	2.9mts	8.97sec.	6.63sec.	3918 mts	178 cm	47 kg	State
134.	8 count	71 count/min	2.21mts	8.87sec.	6.63sec.	3692mts	170cm	48kg	State
135.	10 count	54 count/min	2.30mts	8.75sec.	6.20sec.	3650mts	150cm	37kg	State
136.	12 count	58 count/min	2.35mts	8.82sec.	6.15sec.	3670mts	158cm	34kg	State
137.	15 count	58 count/min	1.68mts	9.67sec.	8.87sec.	2681mts	150cm	52kg	State
138.	16 count	59 count/min	1.72mts	10.45sec.	9.20sec.	2696mts	155cm	53kg	State
139.	18 count	55 count/min	1.75mts	10.50sec.	9.18sec.	2690mts	168cm	51kg	State
140.	9 count	50 count/min	1.70mts	10.48sec.	6.40sec.	3600mts	165cm	52kg	State
141.	8 count	59 count/min	2.56mts	8.20sec.	7.20sec.	3750mts	175cm	62kg	National
142.	4 count	53 count/min	1.88mts	9.31sec.	7.13sec.	3555mts	155cm	41kg	National
143.	9 count	62 count/min	2.46mts	8.90sec.	7.40sec.	3690mts	175cm	82kg	National
144.	10count	65 count/min	2.55mts	8.30sec.	7.10sec.	3720mts	165cm	46kg	National
145.	9count	61 count/min	2.58mts	8.32sec.	7.15sec.	3730mts	170cm	56kg	National

(Contd...)

1	2	3	4	5	6	7	8	9	10
146.	23 count	56 count/min	1.73mts	9.26sec.	8.63sec.	2900mts	149cm	46kg	National
147.	22 count	56 count/min	1.69mts	9.92sec.	9.08sec.	2704mts	157cm	44kg	National
148.	11 count	63 count/min	2.60mts	8.25sec.	7.13sec.	3745mts	150cm	45kg	National
149.	20 count	45 count/min	1.70mts	9.35sec.	9.06sec.	2750mts	163cm	54kg	National
150.	21 count	50 count/min	1.68mts	9.40sec.	9.08sec.	2765mts	153cm	44kg	National
151.	16 count	44 count/min	2.36mts	8.47sec.	7.18sec.	3824mts	167cm	49kg	International
152.	18 count	68 count/min	2.74mts	8.30sec.	6.97sec.	3800mts	168cm	47kg	International
153.	15 count	65 count/min	2.70mts	8.25sec.	6.90sec.	3830mts	168cm	63kg	International
154.	14 count	60 count/min	2.2.80mts	8.25sec.	6.85sec.	3840mts	170cm	54kg	International
155.	26 count	53 count/min	1.75mts	9.30sec.	8.30sec.	2925mts	165cm	49kg	International
156.	27 count	55 count/min	1.72mts	9.40sec.	8.25sec.	2910mts	165cm	55kg	International
157.	25 count	52 count/min	1.55mts	9.35sec.	8.56sec.	2920mts	163cm	60kg	International
158.	32 count	70 count/min	1.73mts	9.58sec.	8.29sec.	2937mts	150cm	46kg	International
159.	28 count	58 count/min	1.65mts	9.59sec.	8.32sec.	2940mts	166cm	60kg	International

(Contd...)

1	*2*	*3*	*4*	*5*	*6*	*7*	*8*	*9*	*10*
160.	24 count	50 count/min	1.70mts	9.60sec.	8.40sec.	2935mts	163cm	55kg	International
JUDO									
161.	12 count	43 count/min	2.46mts	8.31sec.	5.82sec.	3720mts	172cm	59.60kg	District
162.	5count	48 count/min	2.01mts	10.06sec.	7.63sec.	3189mts	159cm	52.30kg	District
163.	9count	33 count/min	2.16mts	9.02sec.	6.53sec.	2953mts	171cm	58kg	District
164.	14count	46 count/min	2.16mts	8.51sec.	6.09sec.	3490mts	163cm	59kg	District
165.	13count	49 count/min	2.34mts	8.72sec.	6.32sec.	3270mts	160cm	57kg	District
166.	11count	42 count/min	1.98mts	8.90sec.	6.59sec.	3189mts	163cm	47kg	District
167.	13 count	35 count/min	1.70mts	10.20sec.	8.64sec.	2280mts	155cm	52kg	District
168.	11 count	36 count/min	1.63mts	9.87sec.	7.06sec.	2644mts	155cm	49kg	District
169.	9 count	33 count/min	1.55mts	9.43sec.	7.44sec.	1071cm	160cm	57.30kg	District
170.	14 count	42 count/min	1.78mts	10.25sec.	8.48sec.	2594mts	160cm	70kg	District
171.	9count	50 count/min	2.31mts	8.79sec.	6.64sec.	3368mts	163cm	60kg	State
172.	10count	47 count/min	2.44mts	8.51sec.	6.90sec.	3650mts	161cm	56kg	State

(Contd...)

1	2	3	4	5	6	7	8	9	10
173.	8count	51 count/min	2.33mts	8.66sec.	7.03sec.	3428mts	154cm	40kg	State
174.	5count	41 count/min	2.23mts	9.50sec.	7.46sec.	2926mts	174cm	81kg	State
175.	9count	50 count/min	2.23mts	9.60sec.	8.40sec.	2217mts	176cm	100kg	State
176.	11count	41 count/min	2.21mts	8.62sec.	6.04sec.	3416mts	155cm	56.60kg	State
177.	22 count	62 count/min	2.16mts	8.90sec.	7.86sec.	2972mts	155cm	57kg	State
178.	19 count	52 count/min	1.98mts	9.78sec.	8.17sec.	2644mts	155cm	48kg	State
179.	17 count	48 count/min	1.92mts	10.60sec.	8.71sec.	2622mts	151cm	48kg	State
180.	18 count	48 count/min	2.1mts	9.87sec.	8.51sec.	2644mts	159cm	63kg	State
181.	21count	52 count/min	2.57mts	8.41sec.	6.37sec.	3190mts	162cm	45kg	National
182.	16count	56 count/min	2.39mts	8.48sec.	6.76sec.	3420mts	162cm	56kg	National
183.	13count	48 count/min	2.18mts	9.15sec.	6.94sec.	3356mts	164cm	55kg	National
184.	11count	51 count/min	2.18mts	9.07sec.	6.76sec.	3375mts	163cm	50kg	National
185.	29 count	64 count/min	2.21mts	8.65sec.	6.93sec.	3650mts	159cm	52kg	National
186.	20 count	28 count/min	2.18mts	9.32sec.	8.10sec.	3543mts	152cm	44kg	National

(Contd...)

1	2	3	4	5	6	7	8	9	10
187.	23 count	54 count/min	2.1mts	9.44sec.	8.20sec.	2842mts	153cm	44kg	National
188.	25 count	57 count/min	1.81mts	8.65sec.	7.50sec.	2944mts	152cm	52kg	National
189.	23 count	48 count/min	1.93mts	9.57sec.	7.73sec.	3116mts	151cm	48kg	National
190.	22 count	44 count/min	2.6mts	9.56sec.	8.36sec.	2157mts	150cm	48kg	National
191.	24 count	60 count/min	2.67mts	8.29sec.	6.41sec.	3950mts	173cm	48kg	International
192.	25 count	62 count/min	2.70mts	8.25sec.	6.39sec.	3890mts	168cm	5[illegible]	International
193.	23 count	63 count/min	2.75mts	8.20sec.	6.35sec.	3855mts	165cm	55kg	International
194.	21 count	60 count/min	2.68mts	8.23sec.	6.35sec.	3780mts	170cm	50kg	International
195	40 count	58count/min	2.11mts	9.22sec.	6.94sec.	2990mts	163cm	45kg	International
196	39 count	58 count/min	2.13mts	9.20sec.	6.90sec.	2980mts	160cm	43kg	International
197	35 count	57 count/min	2.09mts	9.23sec.	6.95sec.	2700mts	163cm	40kg	International
198	30 count	59 count/min	2.25mts	9.10sec.	6.70sec.	2850mts	163cm	45kg	International
199	29 count	58 count/min	2.20mts	9.13sec.	6.75sec.	2940mts	160cm	48kg	International
200	27 count	57 count/min	2.15mts	9.15sec.	6.78sec.	2890mts	160cm	47kg	International

(Contd...)

APPENDIX - E

STEN NORMS PORFORMA

FACTOR	1	2	3	4	5	6	7	8	9	10
Anxiety	0	1	2-3	4-5	6-9	10-14	15-18	19-23	24-26	27-36
Stress	0-6	7-8	9-10	11-12	13-15	16-18	19-20	21-23	24-27	28-36
Depression	0-2	3-4	5-6	7-9	10-12	13-16	17-20	21-26	27-29	30-36
Regression	0-1	2-4	5-8	9-10	11-13	14-17	18-20	21-24	25-26	27-36
Fatigue	0-2	3	4-6	7-10	11-13	14-18	19-22	23-28	29-31	32-36
Guilt	0	1	2	3-4	5-8	9-11	12-16	17-20	21-23	24-36
Extraversion	0-6	7-9	10-11	12-15	16-18	19-21	22-24	25-27	28-31	32-36
Arousal	0-6	7-9	9-12	13-16	17-19	20-23	23-24	25-27	28-31	32-36

Average- 5, 6, Slightly deviant- 4 (Lower Average), 7 (Higher Average), Strongly deviant- 2, 3 (Strongly Lower Average); 8, 9 (Strongly Higher Average) and Extreme 1 or 10.

APPENDIX - F

RAW SCORE NORMS FOR PULL-UPS

Repeatation	Performance Level
15 Above	Excellent
11-14	Good
7-10	Average
3-6	Fair
0-2	Poor

RAW SCORE NORMS FOR SIT-UPS (BENT KNEES)

Repeatation	Performance Level
53-62	Excellent
47-52	Good
39-46	Average
26-38	Fair
1.60 mts.	Poor

RAW SCORE NORMS FOR SHUTTLE RUN

In Second	Performance Level
8.6	Excellent
9.2	Good
9.8	Average
10.4	Fair
11.7	Poor

RAW SCORE NORMS FOR 50 METRE DASH

In Second	Performance Level
6.0	Excellent
6.3	Good
6.6	Average
7.0	Fair
7.7	Poor

RAW SCORE NORMS FOR 12 MINUTE RUN/WALK

Fitness Level	*Low*			*Moderate*			*High*			*Very High*		
% Max. Heart Rate	50	60	65	70	74	77	81	85	88	90	92	100

BODY MASS INDEX KEY FOR HEIGHT AND WEIGHT

< 18.5	Underweight
18.5 to 24.9	Healthy
25 to 29.9	Overweight
30 to 34.9	Grade 1 obesity
35 to 39.9	Grade 2 obesity
> 40	Grade 3 (Morbid obesity)

■Asians are at risk with a BMI>23. Pacific Islanders are risk with a BMI>26.

APPENDIX - G

GLOSSARY OF TEST STATISTICS

t-test for difference of two means

Under the null hypothesis that the two sample means do not differ significantly, then the test-statistic is given by

$$t = \frac{\bar{x} - \bar{y}}{s\sqrt{\frac{1}{n_1} + \frac{1}{n_2}}}$$

follows student's t-distribution with $(n_1 + n_2 - 2)$ degrees of freedom.

Where $\bar{x}$ and $\bar{y}$ are the sample means of sizes n_1 and n_2 respectively and 's' is given by.

F-test (ANOVA): Under the null hypothesis that the sample means do not differ significantly, then the test-statistic is given by

$F = S_t^2 / S_e^2$, follows Snedececer'S F (central) distribution with (k-1, N-k) degrees of freedom.

Where S_t^2 is the mean sum of squares due to treatment (levels/games) and s_e^2 is the mean sum of squares due error.

Levene's test: A test for homogeneity of variance that is insensitive to departures from normality. If the kth observation in the jth of 'm samples be denoted by y_{jk} and if the mean of the n_j observations in this sample be denoted $\bar{y}_j$. We define z_{jk} by

$$zjk = \left| y_{jk} - \bar{y}_j \right|$$

with the mean of the z-values in the jth sample being denoted by z_j and the overall mean of the nz-values being $\bar{z}$. Levene's test statistic (W) is given by

$$W = \frac{n-m}{m-1} \frac{\sum_{j=1}^{m} nj(\bar{z}_j - \bar{z})^2}{\sum_{j=1}^{m} \sum_{k=1}^{mj} (Z_{jk} - \bar{z}_j)^2}$$

If the hypothesis of equality of variance is correct, then the distribution of W is approximately an F-distribution with (m – 1, n – m) degrees of freedom.

P-Value: The probability value, or significance level, from a hypothesis test. 'P' is the probability of the data (or some other more extreme data) arising by chance when the null hypothesis is true.

Index

■■■